DAWN
TO
DUSK

DAWN
TO
DUSK

Memories of a Rural Girlhood

Susie Miles Eutsey

To order additional copies of this book, contact:
Xlibris Corporation
1-888-795-4274
www.Xlibris.com
Orders@Xlibris.com
15697

CONTENTS

Acknowledgements 11

Prelude 13

Chapter I
Country Town, Family House, and Farm Land 15

Chapter II
Living Of The Land 29

Chapter III
Farm Management 45

Chapter IV
Growing Up On The Farm 56

Chapter V
Country Critters 68

Chapter VI
Economy and Politics 71

Chapter VII
Religious Education, Inspirational
and Social Activities 76

Chapter VIII
Uncles and Aunts That Lived Away From Home 83

Chapter IX
Back In The Fall Of Our lives. 91

Chapter X
An End and A New Beginning 104

Epilogue 109

In memory of my Grandmother
Mary Cox Walker

There is no truer and more abiding

Happiness than the knowledge that one

Is free to go on doing, day by day, the

Best work one can do, in the kind one likes best,

And that this works is absorbed by a steady

Market and thus supports one's own life.

Perfect freedom is reserved for the man who

Lives by his own work and in that work

Does what he wants to do.

__ R. G. Collingwood

To my children, grand children, and great grand children

I hope this book will help you to better comprehend the

Lives and labor of your ancestors.

ACKNOWLEDGEMENTS

I am grateful to Former President, Jimmy Carter for his professional expertise for taking me back down memory lane, through reading his book, "An Hour Before Daylight," this help stimulate my thinking and broke through mental roadblocks. We share similar farm experiences.

Special thank you to: *www.whitehouse.gov/presidents,* compiled by The White House. I am grateful for the support I received from: Patricia Crawford, Gene Logsdon, and Sue Robishaw, Homesteading. John Vince, Old Farms; Paul Heiney, Country Life; Karl Schwenke, Living on The Land, James Underwood Crockett, Vegetables and Fruits and M. Peter Hoffman, Cattle, . . . Hogs, and Food, World Book Online Americas Edition.

> http://www.aolsvc.worldbook.aol.com/
> http://*www.newdeal.feri/org/accc.index.htm;*
> http://*www.wpamurals.com/*
> http://*us.history,wisc.edu/hist102/lectures/lecture22.html.*

I owe my deepest thanks to Aleks Grelienska, Nicole Mercurio, and Brian Jang at Xlibris for their guidance to a finished product in publishing my book.

Thanks to J. Wendell Mapson, Jr., The Ministry of Music In The Black Church; and finally, my deepest gratitude belong to my family: To my sister, Doreather McNabb, my brother, Rozell Miles, my husband, Haywood Eutsey, Jr., and my first cousin James E. Gamble who helped me to remember my story. We all shared this memory of living of the land, in the Southern State of Alabama, known as the "Heart of Dixie." I swell with pride, as I write this book "Dawn to Dusk."

I had planned to write a book soon after I retired, but procrastination sat in. I have done my best to recount the episodes during the dawning of my life. My work, my perseverance, my dreams are blessed because our thoughts directly connected.

PRELUDE

Dawn to Dusk is not only an arousing and vibrant story of a true family growing up in the Deep South from 1935 to 1948 but a prose, predicated on the memories of a young girl growing up in a country town on her grandmother's farm, in Mount Andrews, Alabama. Even though she now deceased, she laid the ground work, spiritual and social foundation for our lives. Reflect the southern way of living and lifestyle.

Set in motion by certain factual acts, this biography/autobiography displays the connections between history, agriculture, and post "The Great Depression Era." How family survived and how it extends the branches of the families that populated the Southern State.

From 1935 to 1948 this is a credible story of my experience on how we were raised, worked on the farm, and "living off the Land." I tried to describe the land, house, what growing up on the farm was like and how farming was managed and grandmother skills to raised crops, livestock, pigs, poultry, vegetable in the 30's and 40's without Farm machinery.

Emphasis placed on growing up on the farm and what we encountered in farm life. How we worked, made our own fun, church and school life, our playmates and cousins, along with my brother and two sisters. Our mother deceased in the early thirties, she left four small children, one son, and three girls. After some circumstances beyond our control, we moved from Tuskegee to Mount Andrews, Alabama with our Grandmother, a widow, aunts and uncles, who helped raised us. Grandmother was a well known farmer with the power to own and operate a large farm in the south.

The Walker's Farm surrounded by varieties of trees, pastures and streams, is best known for its corn, cotton, peanuts and livestock, that help to keep this farm alive during 30's 40's and 50's.

These days, new books dealing with all sorts of subject pour from printing presses in an over-whelming cascade. Even if we did nothing but read, we couldn't keep up with the out put, so we must discriminate and decide what we will read and what we will ignore.

I believe "Dawn to Dusk," will garner high readership and the masses will buy it.

CHAPTER I

Country Town, Family House, and Farm Land

Mount Andrews, Alabama a farm town located in Barbour County between Midway and Clayton, Alabama, South East of Union Spring, AL approximately 28 miles from Grandmother's farm, and 13 miles from Clayton, AL. Sixty miles from Tuskegee, AL; take 29 South to Union Springs to 82 East to 51 South take through Mount Andrews to Clayton. At Mount Andrews take a right onto route 25, this will take you to the houses and farmland.

As you turn off the main dirt road onto a more narrower dirt road, through the woods, that lead to a white sandy road opened up to a large six room house that sit off the road, surrounded with farm land and trees. On each side the road was lined with small trees and bushes. A few plumb trees and bullet vines intermingle. To the left there was a long ditch or gully where we played at times.

The Walker's farm encompass 260 acres of farm and swamp land, maybe more or less. This was not flat land, we had hills and valleys throughout the farm. Woods surrounded the farm consist of variety of hardwood including: oak, hickory, black walnut, and a few sweet-gum trees.

The family house guarded by a white fence, shaded by a big magnolia tree that stood by the front gate. It had a perfectly manicured yard with white sand out front.

We had a large front porch. Inside the house was a short hallway with rooms located on each side. The hallway led into a back porch. There were rooms on each side of the porch. The central features of the house were two rock chimneys built on the outside at each end of the house and two fireplaces, one on each end of the house. One in the main bedroom and sitting room, where we sat around the fireplace and where some of the family members slept at night. The other chimney and fireplace were in the "company's room" where our guest slept and where we entertained our boy friends when we were growing up. Directly in front of the back porch was a short walkway to the kitchen, that sit high upon cinder blocks at all four corners. It seems to have been added on and not build when the house was built.

The family kitchen where our food was prepared and cooked. Our eating table was a big rectangle wood table placed almost in the middle of the kitchen with two benches. The benches were on the long side of the table, at the end were chairs. We were allowed to help set the table prior to eating. A smaller table to left that hold drinking water, drawn from the "well" in water buckets. The cook stove was to the left sat near the door that facing the well. A big wooden box kept behind the stove for stove wood cut for cooking. Also, there was a place behind the cook stove for hanging pots and frying pans. A cupboard to the right that held our china ware, like plates, saucers, drinking glasses, sugar bowl, etc. There were shelves right of the eating table where grandmother kept her canned fruits and preserves in jars. Finally, we had to kitchen safe that held more dishes.

Family discussions were done around the kitchen table, also around the fire place where more discussions took place, whether it was about farm work, school work or other type of discipline. A door to the left from the kitchen led to the "well" where we drew our water for drinking, cooking, bathing, washing clothes and so on. We used a "gourd" for a dipper to drink water from, and a bucket used in drawing water. This "well" was surrounded by three large fig trees. Which I enjoyed very much when the figs were ripe.

We did not have an indoor toilet, sink, or bathtub. At the end of the back yard, down the hill a ways sat an "outhouse." When the outhouse was occupied, we used the fields, and wiped with any paper available, or corncobs. In the house at night we used a "slop jar" or "chamber pot" we called it. We took it outside the next morning to dump it in a near by field. We had yard inside and outside the fence that we kept clean. The yards were swept with homemade brooms. Flowers added beauty to the front of the house, roses zinnias, and sunflowers. The sunflowers goes to sleep at night and open up again the next morning. We also, had some slowly developing wild flowers around the edge of the yard and fields. Potted plants adorned the front porch. We had a flower pit in the front yard to the left, where we kept our plants, during the winter to protect them from the cold weather.

A big mulberry tree stood in the backyard, near the smoke house, where we kept cured meat.

There were several shelters around the house. An old T-Model Ford that were not being used; in another shelter, "leather buggy" inside not being used. I used them for my "playhouse." I also, had a playhouse at the edge of the woods in front of the house, where I made mud pies. Sometime I would take my cousins to my playhouse.

To the right of the house was a barn, stable where our two mules, "Queen and Nell" were kept. We also, kept hogs, sows there in separate stalls. Hay, fodder and dried corn, were kept in another part of the barn to feed the animals. There was an upstairs over the stable that also house food for our livestock. Another crib standing by itself with more food for the animals, it was across from the stable. Grandmother had a new crib built in front of the house that sat on the side of the road that lead to the family house.

It seems like we were the center hub of other farmers. On the front left was Elijah and Costella Haslam farm; to the front right was John and Alma Cox farm; almost parallel to the right was Jim and Lessie McNabb's farm; to the left of us was Boss, Stella and Jet Foster's farm; and Sam Scovil's farm was directly behind our farm, over the hills and through the woods. We were relative to most of the farmers that surround us, except the Fosters, and McNabbs. The Foster's had a small country store we used to slip away and buy some goodies. The Simmons farm was down the road to the right of us were also relatives.

Trees. Tree is the largest of all plants. Many trees also live longer than other plants. Some trees live for thousands of years. They are the oldest known living things. People do not think of trees the way they think of other plants, most of which grow only a short time and then die. People think of trees as permanent part of the landscape. Year after year, large, old trees shade houses and streets from the sun. They buds and flower are a sign of spring each year, and their colorful leaves brighter in autumn in many areas.

A tree differs from other plants in four main ways: (1) Most trees grow at least 15 to 20 feet tall. (2) They have a woody stem, which is called a "trunk." (3) The stem grows at least 3 or 4 inches thick. (4) A tree's stem can stand by itself. Our house was surrounded by trees of all types. There are thousands of kinds of trees. But the most trees belong to one of two main groups ~ the broad leaf trees and the needle leaf trees. Trees are very important. For thousands of years, trees have provided people with foods, fibers, and medicines. Above all, they have provided people with wood for use inside and outside the home. Prehistoric people used wood to make the first spear, the first boat, and the first wheel. Throughout history, people have used wood to make tools, constructing buildings, and create works of art. We have used it for fuel to help keep us warm. This is part of country living. Living trees are as valuable to humankind as are tree products because they help conserve natural resources. For instance, wood products each year, loggers cut down millions of trees on the world's forests, like grandmother did. Logs from these trees are shipped to "Sawmills" and" pulp mills." Grandmother had a sawmill on her property a few times. Sawmills cut the logs into lumber, which the building industry uses for many types of construction work. Manufacturers used lumber to make everything from furniture to baseball bats. Pulp mills break down the logs into wood pulp, the main raw material for making paper. The chemical industry uses wood pulp to make alcohol, plastic, and other products. So you see the wood that cut from our land was taken in all directions.

Lumber is another wood product, which includes boards and large pieces of wood that have been sawed from logs. Almost every house uses at least some lumber in its construction and repair. Our family house, barns, cribs, and shelters were made out of lumber, and any repair work around farm house we used lumber. Lumber furnished material from framing, flooring, siding, woodwork, doors, and other building parts.

About fourth is used in building remodeling and repair. The rest goes from sawmills to factories that make boxes, crates, furniture, tool handles, toys and hundred of other products. Sawdust and bark are often used for fuel.

I vaguely remember while we were small, a "saw mill" came to grandmother's land to cut "timber," they cut mostly pines trees. I understand that it takes approximately twenty to twenty five years for trees to grow back and be ready for cutting. Timber has been cut a few times since we left home and monies from the timber were divided among the living off-springs of Wilson and Mary Walker. We stood in the front yard and watched the saw mill trucks move in on the land to cut the timber that they bargain to cut.

From the site where trees were cut, men began "snaking logs" to the truck to load. Logs were then taken to the "plainer mill" to be planed. From lumber houses, schools, churches, large building, and many things were built. We were not allowed to go near the sawmill while they were at work, we just watched the logs as they passed by the house on trucks.

Lumber is divided into two main classes: softwood and hardwood. These classes are not based on the softness or hardness of the wood, rather they refer to the kind of tree from which the lumber came. In cutting down trees, before the loggers go into the woods, the forester decides which trees they should cut. Trees had been marked for cutting. First they make an "undercut," a wedge-shaped piece is cut out off the trunk with an ax or power saw. The faller makes the undercut on the side of the tree that is to fall toward the ground the cut is made close to the ground to avoid wasting valuable wood by leaving a high stump. After the saw has cut through the tree trunk, the undercut makes the tree lose its balance and fall toward that side. Expert fallers can drop a tree exactly where they want it. They can avoid striking other trees, or hitting stumps that might break or damaged the trunk of the falling tree. It consist of two operation. First, the logger skid (drag or haul) the logs to a landing central place in the woods. Second, transporting logs from the landing to the sawmill. Like food products, people in Alabama, and throughout the world eat fruits, nuts and other trees products.

Wilson and Mary Walker, Grandfather and Grandmother.

Wilson and Mary Cox Walker. Wilson Walker was born about October 1866, in Alabama, the son of slave parents, Sam and Omelia Walker. He married about 1895, and deceased in 1930 in Alabama. Mary Cox was born in December 1876 in Alabama, she was the daughter of slave parents, Gamble and June Cox.(1810 Census list her as a Mulatto). She deceased in Birmingham, Alabama, March 5, 1967 at the age of 91. From this union eleven siblings were born. Horace, Lillie, Armiller, Lessie (our mother), Freader, Ethel, Versey, Larcenia, Adolph, Alve, and Alfedo Walker. Today, all siblings are deceased. Aunt Versey lived the longest, she deceased in 2001.

Our mother and father, Lester Miles and Lessie Walker were married in 1923. From this union four children were born: Rozell, Ethel Mary, Dorather, and Susie B., in that order of birth. Our family moved from Louisville, Alabama to Tuskegee Institute, Alabama while I was still a baby. The place were father and mother lived was behind Saint Mark Missionary Baptist Church, where they did light farming. I believe this was located off Montgomery Highway. Tuskegee was predominately a black town and community. Most everything was run by blacks. Most whites lived in the suburbs of Tuskegee. Tuskegee Institute National Historic site in Tuskegee, Alabama included the campus of Tuskegee Institute. The name since that time has changed to Tuskegee University. Founded by Booker T. Washington in 1888 as a vocational school for blacks. Despite of it's humble beginning, Tuskegee gained the support of wealthy and influential donors.

Later the school had become international known. Rozell and Ethel attended Tuskegee Public School. Doreather and I being the youngest were still at home. Our mother deceased in 1932. I was 2 or 2 ½ years old at the time of her death. I have tried so hard to remember her, but I was too young. I had dreams at times that I saw my mother, when I woke up, it all faded away.

Rozell was born in 1924, Ethel in 1926, Doreather in 1928,

and I was born in 1930. Between the four of us, we were two years or more apart in age. It was my understanding that we stayed in Tuskegee for awhile after our mother's death.

Lester Miles and Lessie Walker
Father and Mother

Later on our father married to Mamie Lou Jackson. He started a second family. To this union seven children were born: Lester Jr., Lucille, Alberta, Bernice, Annie Lois, Alphonso P., and Willie Lawrence Miles. We called our stepmother "new mama" until she told us to stop calling her that. As Mamie started her own family she began to mistreat the four of us. It was noticed by our mother's neighbor, Mrs. Motley, and she wrote a letter to grandmother in Mount Andrews and told her we were not being treated right. Grandmother came to Tuskegee and took all four of us back to Mount Andrews with her. Plus for Mamie, she was an immaculate house keeper and an excellent cook.

Rozel, Ethel, Doreather and Me

This was told to us by our grandmother and aunts. Doreather and I were to small to understand what was going on. Rozell and Ethel were old enough to understand better.

They being the oldest of the four of us, they remember when our mother died. Our mother Lessie came down with "influenza" (flu) that raged in the 30's. She was caught off from home in the rain, the flu turn into pneumonia, she had a relapse and did not make it. Grandmother and other member of the Walker family came to Tuskegee to be with our mother during her crisis.

Daddy came to visit us when he could get someone to bring him to Mount Andrews. As we grew up some, a couple of summers we went to Tuskegee to stay with daddy and Mamie for a week. Daddy gave us money to spend while we were there, and we went to the store not far from the house on Montgomery Highway to buy cinnamon buns, we like them very much. Those cinnamon buns has always stuck in my mind. I think Doreather and I was the only one on these visits? Doreather and I were very close to one another. I was just like a shadow, following her around the house and yard. Not being raised up together with our half brothers and sisters, there are a lack of closeness.

But we did visit one another and call each other occasionally, when we grew up. We enjoyed each other when we were together.

Our Mother and father both deceased in Tuskegee. Daddy died in September 1956. He had a stroke and never fully recovered, and died later. He was buried in Tuskegee Cemetery. Mother was taken back to Center Ridge Baptist Church, our home church in Mount Andrews, to be eulogized and buried in the church cemetery.

Daddy owned several lots of land in Tuskegee and a house. He had a large vegetable garden and small crop, but no big time farming. On one occasion, while I was in Tuskegee on a visits, after father's death I went to the court house and ask the Clerk that I would like to see the documents on how our daddy left his property. I also, asked the Clerk for a copy of our father papers showing he owned the property and who was the beneficiary.

The Clerk researched the record and made me a copy of it. I then made copies and gave it to my brother and two sisters so they will know. The documents stated that the property was left to his wife and all his siblings.

After Mamie deceased there were a little confusion. Her children thought that the house and land belong only to them. I informed them that, he was our father first it included all his siblings. Annie told me that, "now you are pulling rank." We all had a big laugh about that, except Willie Lawrence. After I moved to New Jersey, Annie and Alberta visited occasionally, they lived in North Jersey and we lived in Central New Jersey. The end result after Mamie died. Our youngest brother Willie Lawrence bought us out off the house and land. We all agreed to it and signed papers. Now the house and land belong to him only. After that, the closeness seems to widen between us and Willie Lawrence.

I do not know when we moved to Mount Andrews with grandmother, who was then a "widow." When I came to know myself, I was there with grandmother, my uncles, aunts, brother and two sisters. Grandfather died in 1930 the year I was born. I was 6 months old they tell me.

We were raised on a farm that grandmother owned. She owned her own farm equipments: Green and yellow wagon, made by John Deere, plows, hoes, rakes, hole diggers, two mules named "queen and nell" she owned herd of cattle, hogs, hen house full of chicken, this included roosters and hens.

Plenty fruit trees were on the farm: apple, pears, plum, pecan, walnut, persimmon trees. Scuppernongs that grew on vines, they look like grapes except they were light brown, and very juicy and delicious. We picked blackberries, strawberries, bullets, figs and pomegranates. Grandmother and my aunts made jam, jelly and blackberry pies. Home comfort was one of the most creative part of home farming take place not on the land, but back home in the kitchen. That is canning our fruits, and vegetables. When the autumn days are getting shorter and the cupboard must be stocked for the winter. This is where your fruits and vegetables, and meats are made into the finest food you will ever have tasted. Bread, jam, preserves, wines, cider, nothing beats the taste of food and drink over which you have labored, perhaps for many seasons, and can now enjoy the fruit of our labor. I watched grandmother and aunts canned fruit from our fruit trees, apple, peaches and pears.

As children we shook the fruit trees to make fruit fall on the ground and picked them up in a basket for canning and eating. We had to help peel fruit in preparation for canning. Small peaches were pickled whole and put into jars. We also, shelled many field peas, shuck corn for canning vegetables. Field peas, corn, okra, mix vegetable, like gumbo or soup. We preserved fruits such as: figs, apples, pears, and put them in special jars, grandmother bought especially for canning.

In canning fruits and vegetable, a "pressure cooker" was used, that had a gage on the lid to give the temperature and how long fruits and vegetables should cook. I kept some kind of fruits, nuts, roasted peanuts, or baked potato, apple, and pear in my pocket to eat on. My aunts used to tell me that "you going to eat so much, you will be to poor to tote it." I think I knew what that meant?

Recipes From The Old South

Deep Dish Apple Pie

1 ½ cup of sugar

1 Teaspoon nutmeg

¼ Teaspoon salt

2 Tablespoons butter or margarine

Mix ingredients together turn into ungreased square pan 9x9x2 inches, dot with with butter. Cut pastry into strips, alternate with slice apples. Cover deep dish pie with one crust on the top. Bake until brown. 425 temperature.

Bundt or Layer Cake

5 eggs
2 cups of sugar pinch of salt
Teaspoon of Vanilla and/or Lemon flavor
Beat eggs, butter, sugar and flour together until smooth.
Add salt, vanilla and/or lemon flavor. Set over at 350 cook
for about 1 hour or until brown.

Pound Cake

3 cups of sugar
1 cup of milk
1 lb of butter
1 teaspoon of flavor cooking direction are the same as above
under "Bundt and Layer Cake."

Cookies (Tea Cakes)

3 eggs (depend on how much batter you make)
½ cup of butter; teaspoon of flavor
1 Teaspoon Baking power
2 cups of sugar
Mix all ingredients together. Roll your batter over and over,
sprinkle flour on portion of your table, then take a rolling
pin and roll it out thin, take a drinking glass and cut out into
round cookies. Put cookies in shallow tin pan. Put in oven at
350 degree bake until brown. Sometime you have used
your own judgment, on how much milk to use, depend on
the consistency of the batter.

Peach cobbler

Peaches to fit your baking dish   ½ cup flour, sifted
1/3 cup butter   1 ½ cup of sugar
1 teaspoon of flavor

Peel and halves. Blend other ingredients together well and
place over peaches in oven Roll out batter thin with rolling
pin and spread on top of pan. Cook until crust is brown.

Corn Bread Dressing

2 cups white corn meal	½ teaspoon salt
3 eggs	1 celery heart, chop finely
2 cups of milk	1 onion chopped finely
1 pack of chicken gizzards	½ cup stock cook pack of chicken gizzards and chopped fine.

Make corn bread by combining corn meal, soda, buttermilk,
melted butter, three eggs, ad salt and pepper to taste. Beat
well and bake (in 350-degree oven) until brown or about
30 minutes. Crumble bread and add remaining ingredients.
Bake separately (about 30 minute in 350-degree oven) or
stuff bird as desired. I use 10 inch iron frying pan if dressing
is baked separately?

Being a native of Alabama, many of these old recipes my
grandmother, aunts, sisters, and myself have used for many years.
It is true what they say about Dixie, that it's the home of some of
the finest cooks and most tempting cuisine in these United Sates?
If you have any doubt, just try eating homemade cakes, pies
cobblers, biscuits, and southern fried chicken, cooked in the Deep
South, are bursting with mouth-watering dishes to suit every mood
and every occasion.

CHAPTER II

Living Of The Land

"If ye be willing and obedience, ye shall eat the good of the land"

Isaiah 1:19

Farming is the most important occupation in the world. People cannot live without food, and nearly all the food they eat comes from crop and livestock raised on farms. Various industrial materials, such as cotton and wool also, come from plants and animals raised on the farm.

Owning a farm carries with it responsibilities, not only for the crops you plant and animal you rear, but also for everything that was there before you started to mold the holding to your own needs. The trees, meadows, and ponds, and all their inhabitants from the smallest insect to the largest mammal, were all there before you, and conserving them should be as much a part of your farming as crops and livestock.

Farming was once the chief way of life in nearly every country. For example, the typical American family of the 1700's and early 1800's live on small farm. The family raised cattle, chickens, and hogs and grew corn, fruits, garden vegetable, hay and wheat. Everyone in the worked long and hard, but the results were often disappointing.

Most people produced barely enough food for themselves. The situation began to change during the last half of the 1800's and it changed remarkably during the 1900's.

As farming has become less important as a way of life in the United States, it has become more and more important as a business. Farms that are not run in a business like way have great difficulty surviving. It somewhat like a home based business, where you set your own hours, work hard and long as you see fit. Even with the great decrease in the number of farmers, the nation's farm produce more food than the American people use. This surplus has enable the United States to become the world's chief food exporter. About a sixth of all food export comes from Americans farms.

Most farmers during our time had diversified farms like grandmothers. A typical mixed farm in the South produce beef, cattle, peanuts, hogs, as we did. If you do not do well with farm products, you be able to rely on cattle and hogs. I think this make good planning for farmers. Remember variety is the spice of life. However, we did not raised sheeps, goats, and tobacco on our farm, like they did in other part of the Southland.

Basic principle of crop production requires nutrients (nourishing substances) and water to grow. Good soil supplies most of the nutrients. It also store the water that the crops need. Crops take root in the soil and absorb nutrients and water through their roots. Farmers make sure that the soil and water resources meet the needs of each crop. Most farmers plan their method of soil and water management and of pest control well in advance of the growing season. Soil need to be rich in mineral particle mixed with decaying organic (plant and animal) matter, or compost.

Crops cannot grow without water. In most cases, farmers rely entirely on rainfall for the necessary moisture. On our farm we did not exactly practice "dry farming." In dry farming part of the cropland is left fallow (unplanted) each year. The fallow soil can store moisture for a crop the following year. Grandmother rotated field of some of her crops. For example, if corn or peanuts were planted in one soil area one year the next year she would plant something else there. I suppose that was the reason they change field (soil) in planting season. Grow the same crop on the same piece of land year after year, and soon there will be no crop at all.

A water supply was very basic need for any household. The daily life of the farm house require a considerable amount of water. "Wells" are the oldest form of man's efforts to secure a reliable supply of water, but the work of raising it's bucket one at a time was very slow. We used water when cooking, washing dishes, clothes and taking baths. Our cattle had to be watered, and the hogs. At times we had rainy season. Plants are much like people, they have to be fed watered, and kept from freezing. These are growing plants in warm climate. Remember, we are "living of the land," from our crops, cattle, pigs, poultry, gardening and hunting. We used pesticide to control insects. All pesticide had to be used with extreme care. If they are used improperly, they may pollute the environment or the food supply and so endanger people's health.

Grandmother also, used other methods of pest control in addition to pesticides. Turning the soil with a plow to kill most weeds. Crops farming involves at least five separate operations: (1) preparing the soil (2) planting, (3) cultivating, (4) harvesting, and (5) processing and storage. We did not use tractor equipment to accomplish the task, we used mules and sometimes an oxen. The main purpose of soil preparation is to make a "seedbed" that is, and area of soil in which seeds can be planted and in which they will sprout, take root, and grow. Most farmers make the seedbed by an age-old process called "tillage." Tillage involves digging into the soil and mixing it. Plows are our chief tillage devices. The plows loosens the soil, kills the weeds and improves the circulation of water and air in the soil. I believe grandmother's plows used were steel beam? When plowing, it not only make furrows, it scatters the dead stalks, leaves and other plant waste from the preceding crop help protect soil from erosion. They also, enrich the soil with nutrients if they are plowed under.

Land had to be made ready by breaking ground, for planting. The plow made furrows for farmers to plant the seeds. Good plowing, it has been wisely said, is the basis of good farming. It is the job of the "plow" to turn the soil, allowing the freshly turned earth to be exposed to wind, sun, rain, and air, burying the weeds and the remains of the previous crops; and also placing any fertilizer or manure where the roots of the crop can best get at it. There are a few objects more symbolic of agriculture than the plow. Styles of plowing, and the method of cutting the first furrows, vary according to local custom.

There is no better way to learn the ways of the land, and feel of the soil, than to follow a plow. Plows continue to dominate the scene during our time.

Now is time to plant. Nearly all field crops are planted by planters. The machines cut the furrows (narrow grooves) in the soil, drop seed into each furrow. And cover the seeds with soil, all in one operations. Spreading seeds on the land and expecting a crop in return is one of the greatest act of "faith" in the farming year. We sowed some seeds by hand other were sown by planter. Sowing by hand is older than the old testament and still practiced in some part of the country. Grandmother and our aunts carried seed in their "apron" when sowing by hand.

To grow crops, farmers need fairly level land tillable (workable) soil. In addition the climate must provide a certain amount of warmth and moisture. For example, most crops need frost-free period, or growing season, at least 90 days to development seeds into mature plants. Agriculture is the world's most important industry. It provide us with almost all our food. It also, supplies materials for two other basic human needs, clothing and shelter.

Corn, cotton, and other seeds, sometime seeds were soared with our hand. They are space apart far enough space for the seeds to grow once the seed start to grow, be it corn, cotton or peanut, the crops had to be cultivated, mostly by using a plow to uproot the weed and grass so it will die, and sometime we would hoe around what's planted to get the grass close up. In field where row crops are grown, weeds can multiply rapidly between rows.

Once the crop matured, it stop growing. Come fall, is harvesting time. Harvesting was always a serious matter. For the farmer it was one of those critical times of the year when they knew that the season's fortunes were dependent upon the weather.

Harvesting formed an important part of the family budget. Good yield are an integral part of good farming practices. All field crops are not gathered by machines. All of grandmother's harvest were done manually.

Crops raised to supply food for human being are called food crops. This includes: canned goods, like field peas, corn, fruits from fruit trees, canned and preserved are storage. Crops we preserve for livestock: hay, fodder, dried corn, are also storage in our barns, and cribs, for our animals. Grandmother, did like many farmers, rotate her crop from year to year. To reduced the need for chemical fertilizers. This is similar to the method I mention about the soil moist, when it do not get enough rain.

Grandmother owned her own farm, unlike some farmers had to rent all or part of their land. Farmers that rent all their land, were called "tenant farmers." While yet other farmers did sharecropping. The joys of growing your own, you certainly get freshness and you may also save some money. But then you may not. You can beat the store prices every time, when you stop to add the cost of fertilize, pesticide, tools, and other odds and ends (including your own labor) you will be lucky to break even. No matter, you will enjoy several things money cannot buy, including the unique satisfaction of growing precisely what you want and eating it at it's prime. You can experience at first hand the age-old miracle of tiny seeds becoming bountifully producing plant

And too, a little spading, hoeing and weed pulling never hurt anyone's waistline. I want to discuss fruit trees on the land. I mention that we had apple, peach, and pear trees under farm management or growing up on the farm. Here I want to be more descriptive on fruit trees. Apple is one of the most important fruits that grow on trees. It also, one of the most popular of all fruits. Since prehistoric times, people have enjoyed the delicious flavor of apples. There are hundreds of varieties of apples.

Their color range from various shades of red to green and yellow
and their flavor varies from tart to sweet. Apple trees belong to the
rose family. Their beautiful white flowers open in spring and look
like tiny roses. Over half the apple grown are eaten fresh. Apples
also are baked into pies and many other dishes. They are used in
making apple butter, apple juice, applesauce, jelly and wine. Most
apple products are canned or bottled, and other dried or frozen.

From apple trees we make apple pies, apple fritters, cobblers,
jelly, jam and preserves. Grandmother and my aunts have made all of
those mention above. Trees need to be watered, fertilized and pruned.
Usually, we fertilized the roots of the trees and prune the trees in the
spring of the year. Pruning is the cutting away of plant parts, such as
branches, shoots, buds, or roots. Pruning serves various functions. It
help plants recover from the shock of being moved. It controls the
shape and appearance of plants. Pruning also contribute to the size,
quantity and quality of fruit. Trees will yield, fruit Quality and fruit
size are directly proportional to the time you showed on it. As a
grower and farmer you perform the same task no matter what size
the tree.

Location, location, location as in Real Estate, so it is with gardening
and farming. Most of our fruit trees are in the field around the house,
some were out on the terrain (except the fig and mulberry trees, that
were in the back yard), on a slope and some were in low areas. Dirt is
not soil, dirt is what you find on a finger of a five year old hand. Soil
contributes to the climate for tree growth by supplying tree with air,
water, nutrients and organic matter.

Peach is roundish, yellow to reddish, edible fruit. It has a hard,
deeply pitted stone. Peaches are ripen from early summer to fall,
some as late as October. Peaches, have skin with a partition that
make it easy to split. Grandmother raised two kinds of peaches:
Clingstone and Freestone. Clingstone peach, stones are ribbed or
perforated with small holes in the shell. We call it the core of the
peach. Clingstone the flesh clings to this shell. Freestone the fruits are
free and easier to enjoy without having to tease it off the stone.

Clingstone peaches were at it's best canned whole and sometime pickled, where freestone sliced and canned. With freestone peach you did not have to cut it open, you could pull it apart with your hand, as opposed to clingstone you had to either used a knife are bite it with your teeth. Freestone peaches is usually softer than that of clingstones.

Peaches are good to eat right from the tree. From peaches we get: peach pies, cobbles, canned peaches and pickled peaches. We help our aunt peel peaches and put a little sugar on them and cook them down low. This is good with hot home made biscuit. We did the same thing with tomatoes. Which will be discussed in the garden section.

Pear is a fleshy fruit. Some pears are large and round at the blossom end and taper inward toward the stem. Other may be almost completely round, like an apple. The pear tree is closely related to the apple tree. The fruit is covered with a smooth, thick skin, which may be yellow, russet, or red. It's juicy flesh is sweet and mellow. It is also tender, through tiny, hard grit cells make the flesh of some pears taste sandy. Pears are used widely as a dessert fruit. About half of all pears grown are eaten fresh. But many are canned alone or in combinations with other fruits. Some pears are dried. Grandmother and our aunts made pear preserved, and was very good. I personally ate pears right off the tree, like apples and peaches.

The red mulberry tree, we did not pick and cook mulberries. However, I ate a few mulberries from the tree that was located in our back yard. I believe the birds and chicken also ate mulberries. We also, ate scuppernong, that grow on a vine. Grandmother had them where their vines would run upon a pole and across the top of the wood frame she had built.

Corn, Cotton and Peanuts.

Corn also called maize, is plant whose food value and wide variety of uses make it the most important crop grown in the United States. It is also one of the most important crop in the world. In order of world grain production, corn ranks second, after wheat and rice is third. Those three grains are the chief source of energy in the human diet. To grow corn give the land lots of good manure, and the corn will love it.

You do not need tropical heat to grow corn, you need rich soil and warmth. Corn will not germinate unless the temperature warm enough. The greatest threat to the young corn is birds especially crows. Corn contain plenty of protein, and apart from its value as a human food, it is excellent fodder for nearly all farm animals.

Corn has an amazing number of uses. The "kernel" that is the corn grain, or seed can simply be cooked and eaten. Corn, cornstalks and other part of corn plants, are fed to livestock. We ate corn in a variety of ways, we enjoyed eating sweet corn on the cob, after the ears have been boiled or roasted. Corn kernels that have been removed from the cob and fried, we call that "roshanell." We like fresh yellow and white corn best when it tender just pulled from the corn stalk, desilked (remove the corn silk), washed and fried. Corn grain is especially rich in starch. Starch is a carbohydrate, a nursing substance in food that provides the body with energy. But corn protein lack some of the important chemical unit called "amino acids" that the body needs.

There are many kinds of corn, but I will just mention three: (1) field corn for animals, (2) sweet corn for human, (3) popcorn. Corn is the "king" in this country. Culture is practically the same for all three. Most types of corn have a growing season of four to six months, usually beginning in Aril or early May. We were like much of the world, our corn we grown on a large farm. The harvesting of corn begins when the moisture content of the mature kernel dried enough.

Harvesting may take place as early as August, sometime September. All our harvest was done manually, except some aspect of peanuts. I will discuss this under peanuts. From our corn field, grandmother took dried corn to Clayton, Alabama to corn meal grinder, to make meal, to bake corn bread, and corn muffins. Grits could also be made from corn. She bought flour to make biscuits, cakes, pies pie crusts, and tea cakes cookies.

We pulled dried corn ears, and pulled the brown leaves from the corn stalk, bundle it, wrapped it with one of its leave, we called this "fodder," and hauled it all off in our wagon to the barn and cribs, for our livestock and hogs to feed on during the year. Corn grains was used to product alcohol, and corn was one of the ingredient in "moonshine" whiskey. This was quite prevalent in Southern States, call "boot leg" Whiskey, which was illegal. Those caught making it, was sent away to do some time. Cotton, corn and peanuts are such important field crops in the United States many farmers plant them year after year in same or different fields. We planted corn in rows wide enough to allow for whatever kind of cultivation that you intended to use. Think we planted about 2 feet apart. As the corn begin to grow, we sprinkle it with a white fertilizer called "soda" to help it grow. We always plowed our corn with a plow.

Cotton, was picked with our hands, from the cotton bulbs, and put into a cotton sack, made by Aunt Lillie. She took a guano sack and made straps to sew on the sack, so it will fit over our shoulders, while picking cotton. When the sack was filled with cotton, or heavy enough for us to go to the "basket" and empty our sack. Then we went back to pick more cotton. Grandmother would weigh the cotton right in the field with steelyard to see how much cotton weighed. We need to pick bale of cotton so grandmother, Alfedo, or Rozell would take the bale of cotton to the cotton gin in the wagon to Mount Andrews. There the cotton was weighed again at the cotton gin to determine how much she would get for a bale of cotton, also based on the selling price of cotton at that time. Cotton gin is a machine for removing the seed from cotton fibers. It widely believed that the American Inventor Eli Whitney produced the first cotton gin. His invention has helped make the United States the world's leading cotton grower.

Peanut is a plant species grown mainly for its fruit. The peanut is a member of legume family, that is, it bears fruit in the form of pod (shell) that contain one or more seeds. There are two seeds in most peanut pods. These tasty seeds are also called peanuts. They are a favorite food of mine and many other peoples. They can be eaten alone or mixed into candy, cookies, breads, and pies. Some ice cream is flavored with peanut butter. Peanut bread is rich in proteins and low in starch. Peanuts sometimes sold fresh as well as boiled peanuts. Some farmers, instead of drying the peanut after picking, they wash the peanuts and boiled them in salt water. In cultivation peanuts plants, they need much sunshine, warm temperature, and moderate rainfall, and frost-free growing period of four to five months.

Peanut butter is also a popular food worldwide. It is popular on many school menus. The children call it "PB&J" sandwich for peanut butter and jelly. This one of their most favorite sandwiches in most elementary schools. Peanut are an important crop, especially in the warn regions of the world. In the United States, Georgia Produces more peanuts than any state. Since 1930's peanut yield in the United States has Increased dramatically. In Georgia, for example, the average yield per unit of peanut farmland is about five times greater today than it was in the 1930's.

The peanut plant is usual because its pods develop underground. For this reason, peanuts are often called "groundnuts" or "goobers." Peanuts are a nutritious food.

There are more energy-giving calories in roasted peanuts or peanut butter than in an equal weight of beefsteak. Some uses of peanuts. As food manufacturers roast peanuts inside the pods and sell them as whole roasted-in-shell peanuts. In addition, they remove the shell and roast and sell only the seeds. Like roasted peanut in cans and jars. Some are plain roasted and other salted to improve their flavor. Most shelled peanuts are either oil roasted or dry roasted. Roasted peanuts, and peanut butter is fat, satisfying, and healthy, but should be ate within moderation.

I have discussed how we plant, grow and harvest our peanut under farm management in this book. Corn, cotton, and peanuts were repeated process yearly for the farmers, from planting to harvest.

Cattle, Hog, Poultry and Food

I have discussed briefly, that we had cattle, hog, poultry and food under farm management and growing up on the farm. Here, I will elaborate more on important to us as a people. Cattle are among the most important farm animals. We eat the meat of cattle as roast beef, veal, hamburgers, and hotdogs. We drink the milk of cattle and use in to make butter, cheese, ice cream. The hides of cattle provide leather for shoes.

Cattle also, furnish material for such useful items as medicine, soap, and glue. Cattle supply power by pulling plows, carts and wagon. Cattle chew their food two separate times to digest it. After they chew and swallow the food, they bring it up from the Stomach and chew it again. This once-swallowed food is called a "cud." Cattle are less intelligent than many other domestic animals. People sometimes name them, but cattle rarely learn to respond to their name as horses and dogs do.

Livestock Grazing.

Cattle roam and graze in green pastures and on the plains. Their "mooing" or "lowing" often break the silence of the country side. Grandmother had two cow pastures, and two hogs pastures. When the cows and hogs grazed down on one pasture, they moved to the other pastures of fresh grass. Livestock were confined by pastures and stables. Sometimes pastures were fenced in by barbed wire as a reinforcement. Our cows, bulls, got out off the pasture and mules occasionally go out off the barn yard they wondered around, and we had to help get them back in their prospective places.

To raised livestock successfully, we had to provide the animal with the proper care. Certain animals must be selected for breeding (reproductive) purposed to replace the animals that are marketed or that outgrow their usefulness. Livestock care consist of providing feed and shelter for the animals and safeguarding their health. Most farm animals are raised to provide livestock products. However, also raised breeding stock that is, animals of superior quality used mainly to produced off-springs. Beef cattle are raised for their meat. Dairy cattle are raised for their milk. Dual-purpose cattle provide both meat and milk.

The word cattle usually mean cows, bulls, steers, heifers, and calves. A cow is a female and a bull is a male. Steers are males that have had some of their reproductive organs removed. A young cow is called a heifer until she give birth to a calf. A calf is a young heifer or bull. A group of cattle is known as a "herd." young heifer or bull. Mule is a domesticated, hybrid animal that results from crossing a mare (female horse and a Jack (male donkey).

Mules were popular work animals during our time on the farm. Mule looks somewhat like both its parents. Like the jack, a mule has long ears, short mane, small feet and tail with tuft of long hair at the end. From the mother it gets a large, well-shaped body and strong muscles. A mule is less likely to suffer from overwork than a horse. Mules can remain strong under much harsh treatment and work, but they work better if they are treated with kindness. In the United State, over nine tenth of all mules have worked on farms, and plantations. Most of them have been used in the South.

Dairy. Is the branch of agriculture concerned with the production of milk, butter, evaporate milk and dried milk products. Milk is the nourishing of all foods and favorite drink of people throughout the world. Milk has almost all the nutrients that human beings need for growth and good health.

In addition, milk has most of these nutrients in large amounts and in such proportions that they can work as a team to help keep the body strong and healthy. Carbohydrates are a major source of energy for the body. The carbohydrate content of milk is mainly lactose. Farmers in America are the world's leading producer of cow's milk. As my aunts milk the cows, I was the person that kept the calf away until she finish milking. The milk was taken home. From this milk we made butter, buttermilk, and we kept some milk fresh. My sisters and I had the job of taking turn churning the milk to make butter. As we churned, yellow butter would surface on top of the milk. Our aunts took off the butter and placed it in a container, to mold it. Churned milk became buttermilk. As we grew older, my sister and I learned "how to milk" cows, slopping hogs that's feeding them with scraps from the kitchen. I like to feed the mule hay, fodder and corn.

There is nothing difficult about milking, you only need a stool to sit on and a bucket to catch the milk. Once you start milking a cow, you are stuck with the job until her milk dries up. To milk you squeeze firmly downward on the teats to force milk down and out. Release the teats at once, this will stop the flow of milk. Milking problem, some cows hate being milked and will kick you. Even more irritating are the cows that will wait until the bucket is full, and then kick that. Some cows like to eat while you milk them. When we milk our cows in the field in a cow pen, the milk went from the farm to the table. This called "raw milk," because our milk was not pasteurized.

Carefully planning requires to maintain a year around supply of food for cows. calves have to be kept away from their mother while milking. Calves are eventually wean from their mother. Some calves are self weaning and give up the teat at six months old. Regardless from what might be called minor routine and maintenance, a cow's only request are to be adequately fed and milked. We usually milk the cows once a day.

Hog, is a farm animal raised throughout the world. These animals, provide pork, which is eaten as port chops, ham, bacon, and sausage. Remnants of hogs are used to make a variety of products. Such as, lard, cracklings, souse, chitterlings, pig meat was an important element in our diet. Nothing from the pig was wasted. Both young and adult hogs are also called "pig" or "swine." Young hogs are almost always called pigs. Hogs rank among the most intelligent of the domesticated (tame) animals, some people say they are dirty, yet hogs keep themselves cleaner than most other farm animals do. However, hogs will often wallow (roll about) in mud to cool themselves during warm periods. The pig is a generous animal, giving up to 20 piglets a year. As I mention above do not fall in to the trap thinking pigs are filthy and stupid. Two perfectly reasonable and healthy things account for their grubby image; the way they dig their snout into soil, searching for grubs and worms; and they wallow in mud when there a danger that strong sun will burn their skin. A sow will organize her home by moving around with her snout to make a safe bed for her piglets. Pigs only ask for three things: shelter, space, and something to dig in. If you can provide all three, then your pig will be happy. They also need room to roam and exercise. They will eat most anything if you let them, and will quite happily eat house scraps. But they are vegetarian and should never be given meat. Pigs eat and drink out of a "trough," and graze in pastures. We also, gave them "slop" from the kitchen.

Poultry. Are birds that are raised to provide meat and eggs for human food. Chicken are by far the most common kind of poultry raised throughout the world. Other species include turkeys, guinea fowls, ducks, geese, pheasant, pigeons, and quail. Although we did not raise ducks, geese, pheasants, pigeons, and quails on our farm. We raised chickens, guinea fowls, turkeys. Poultry are used primarily for food, they also provide several important byproducts. Farmers use poultry manure as fertilizer. Poultry keeping can be as large or small an affair as you wish it to be. There are good profits to be made from poultry and eggs produced. The work you do, can be a lot or a little, depending how much you wish to achieve with your birds. Grandmother bought baby chicks to raise and some were hatched right from the hen as she sat on her nest in the henhouse. The hen would sit over nest of eggs for a period of time.

It take one determined fox to destroy a sizable flock of poultry before you even had a chance to get out of bed to see what the noise is all about. Make sure your chicken get plenty of sunshine and room to roam. As a child, I could hear the rooster crowing early in the morning, this was like a wake up call. The hens started singing later on in the day. We had different breeds of chickens: Rhode Island Red, an ancestor of brown eggs, laying hybrid. Light Sussex (white) popular bring forth eggs and meat.

Ancona Batan(speckle) small bird. We had quite a few speckle hens, producing eggs, meat, and manure are essential farm economy. Eggs are small, medium, large, extra large, and jumbo's brown eggs often have double yolk and of excellent quality.

Regardless of the size, I just like scrambled eggs and boiled eggs. Chicken can be prepared in a variety of ways. Fried, stewed, baked, grilled, barbeque, chicken sandwich, to name a few. Laying hens were profitable for grandmother, she took from eleven to twelve dozen to town at once to sell. They are part of our cash crop.

Food. Is one of our most basic needs. We cannot live without it. Food give us the energy for everything we do: walking, talking, working, playing, reading, and even thinking and breathing. Food also provides the energy for our nerves, muscles, heart and glands need to work. Food also does more than help keep us alive, strong, and all living things must have food to live. Green plants use the energy of sunlight to make food out of carbon dioxide and water and other substances from the soil.

Although most of the food we eat comes from plants or animals, the variety of food as marketable. Plants provide such basic foods as grains, fruits, and vegetables.

Animals provide meats and milk. These basic food may require little or no preparation before they are eaten. We ate healthy during our stay with grandmother. We ate solid good food, not junk food. Fresh vegetables, fruits and nuts directly from the trees.

There were no fast food places to eat in those days. A few restaurants around Clayton, which served soul food, fresh cooked vegetable and meats, homemade pies, and cake.

We did not eat at any of them. The people that ate there were the class of people that hung around "juke joints"(bars) and alleys. Travelers came to town looking for a good place to eat from a southern restaurant that served soul food while they were out.

The secret of successful food-raising lies in the soil. If the ground you sow your vegetables, fruits, and grains on is properly conditioned and cared for, your work is half completed. You really do not grow the plants, nature does. Take care of your soil and the plants will take care of you. "The pioneer once said that land that supported large black walnut trees was always good fertile ground." Some farmland will have to be fertilized heavily to get good crops of corn or legumes. Generally speaking land where anything grows extra large and lush, even weeds indicate land potentially good for farming.

Food from the field is undeniable in the sight of a field of flourishing crops, ripening under the summer sun. But there is even greater joy to be had from knowing that it is only through your efforts that soil has been fertilized and duly tilled, the seed sown, the weeds hoed and kept down, the pest deterred, and the plant tended until the food is ready for harvest.

CHAPTER III

Farm Management

There is a woman at the beginning of all good things"

___Lamartine

The Walker's farm was diversified, and require no regular hired help. What follows is based upon experience. After years of farming grandmother must have reached her goal of economic self-sufficiency. Agriculture required hard work, careful planning and thoughtful care. Mechanical operations includes: hoeing, cultivating, plowing, harvesting, spraying and dusting to kill insects, one in particular, "boll-weevil" that damage the cotton bulbs.

During my earliest recollection, the family business was taken care of by the man, even the grocery, that was not raised on the farm was purchased by my grandfather.

When my grandfather died, my grandmother had to assume the responsibility as head of the family. She said she did not have a clue about the business aspect of the farm such as selling what was produced. After her first encounter with business deals, she caught on quickly. She stated that the woman should be involved in the business affairs so that if it becomes necessary, she can rise to the occasion that makes for a smooth transition.

My grandmother became very efficient operating the farm, to the extent that she was envied by some of the men farmers in the community.

Her eldest son, Horace, was instrumental in helping her with difficult decisions. There was always something to do on the farm. We arose early every morning to milk the cows, and feed the farm animals before going of to school that was two miles away. Because buses were not provided for us, we had the pleasure of walking and socializing with other youngster in the community.

Grandmother was a good business manager. She worked with her family to have a good crop. Grandmother did her best because this was not just our life style but our livelihood. Our lives and income depend on the outcome devoted efforts to the maintenance of her farm. The real joy of farming comes from the sight of a table laden with food you have grown yourself and making money from your harvest. That lessen our dependence on the outside world. She eliminated the middle man, farming was a different type of life style, and it was a honest way of life.

In the spring we planted and the fall we reap the harvest. Like picking cotton, pulling corn, and shaking dirt of peanuts. We raised two kinds of peanuts: "spanish" (small) and "runners" (large) peanuts. After the peanut was plowed under, we would shake dirt of the peanuts, heaped them in a pile. I use to get on the wagon as it passed the heaps, and stamped peanuts down, with my feet, as they were thrown on the wagon, so more peanuts could be put on. Two people were on each side of the wagon with pitch fork throwing them on from the pile of peanuts on the ground. At some point, the pitch fork struck my left leg, scraped it and cause it to later fester, that generated pus. Grandmother or one of my aunts took a needle with burnt end and pierce it, so the pus would drain. Then put some mercurochrome or iodine on the wound. I have a permanent scar the size of a nickel on my left leg; now I am marked for life. We then stacked the peanuts on a pole to dry out. The peanuts were left for a few weeks. Uncle Alfedo and Rozell was responsible for going into the woods to cut poles for stacking peanuts.

Our next step was to get a thrasher to come out and thrash the peanut of the poles and grandmother took them to town for sale. At the time peanuts were thrashed, bales of "hay" were made with a compressor by compressing peanuts vines, and leaves into bales of hay, then tired it with wire to hold it together. Hay was used to help feed the livestock. Grandmother, Uncle Alfedo and Rozell took care of dealing with the peanut thrasher and compressor. We kept peanuts on hand, because weeks after thrashing them, my sisters and I picked loose peanuts on the ground. Doreather helped grandmother figure the money then grandmother took some of them to town and sold them for us, and gave us the money for our work.

Another event that was central to country folk was hog slaughtering time. Certain times a year, grandmother would set aside hogs to fatten them for killing.

When time came to kill the hogs my uncles would shoot or cut the hog under the neck and turn it upside down to drained the blood, put them in boiling hot water, this took the hair off and then took the hog hind legs at the bottom and slit it; put a pole in between the hind legs hang it on the gallows and cut it open down the center of the stomach, took out the inside of the hog. The small intestines, were cleaned and used for casing sausages. Certain part of the hog was grinded in a meat grinder. This is how we got our "link" sausage. The sausages that did not go into the casing, we made patty sausages.

Hog head, ears, and jowl made "souse," large, small intestines, and hog maws made "chitterlings." The hog brains were cleaned and scramble with eggs for eating. My aunts made hash from ground meat of the hog; fat was cooked down to make "lard."

The lard was put in containers to use when need for cooking. Pig feet and pig ears were cut off, used for cooking, pig feet were cooked in a variety of ways: boiled, baked, pickled, the same with pig ears. From the outer hog we get: ham, bacon, pork chops, spareribs, pork lion, shoulder, cracklings, and ham hocks. Everyone worked hard and reaped the benefit of their labor. Certain meats like: bacon, sausage, shoulder, ham, were "smoked," salted down and kept in the "smokehouse." When we got ready to eat any of these meats, we would go to the smokehouse and take out the meat we wanted for the day. I did not get to close when most the hogs were killed, because I did not care to see those things, knowing that we had to eat this meat.

The cows breed with the bulls and we had calves. As they grew, most of them were sold for a profit, another cash crop. Occasionally, cows were taken to the slaughter house to be slaughtered, cleaned, cut up and package into reasonable sizes and put in the deep freeze to use as needed for cooking.

Vegetable Garden. Our vegetable garden supply us with fresh vegetables from April until early November. We ate fresh vegetable during the spring, summer and fall months. Winter months we relied on our canned vegetables. You should grow as much vegetables as you can eat or preserved, because you will need and use it later. In our vegetable garden, grandmother produced: snap beans, collard greens, turnip greens, mustard greens, sweet potatoes, Irish potatoes (white), rutabagas (yellow turnips), onions, butter beans, beets, cabbage, black eye peas, crowder peas, speckle peas, sweet peas, okra, squash, cucumbers, eggplants, tomatoes, green peppers, watermelons, cantaloupes, and sometime sweet corn.

We raised a variety of sweet and hot peppers. Plant a plenty of hot peppers, if you like them, they accompany collard greens, and green peas. Cabbage, I like the greener head better than the white head. Some peas and beans are best grown on a fence or trellis, plant them early in the spring. Bush type beans are less trouble. When picking beans cut or pull collard green leaves, this encourage more to develop. Select sweet potatoes from the grocery store, plant them in six inches of sands with three inches of manure under the sand. Keep the sand moist with a plenty of water, and soon potatoes sprout many plants. You can break the shoots from the potato and plant them, make sure you water them the first couples of days after setting them out. The plant will wilt at first, but generally they will come back.

White potatoes, sweet potatoes, turnips and beets are "tuber" plants, because their roots are grown underground, and that the part we eat. Turnips, scallions(onion), we eat both tops and roots. Grandmother, saved some dried seeds from her vegetable garden to replant for the next Spring.

Tomatoes has many varieties, we cook them like we did peaches, put sugar in them while they cooked, and ate them for breakfast with biscuits. Some of our cousins ate tomatoes sprinkle with salt on them and ate them whole like an apple or peach.

Green tomatoes are good just slice them and sprinkle with salt and black pepper, then flour the slices and put them in hot "lard" or fried meat grease, like eggplants.

Eggplants, unlike tomatoes or peppers, eggplants are not sweet or edible raw. The large, purple, glossy, smooth-skinned fruit grow on waist-high stalks. They can be peeled, chopped, sliced, salted and fried them slow and allow them to brown, that's good eating. Eggplants require more care, feeding and watering, than most other vegetables. Okra, the more common are "lady fingers" and "gumbo," okra is good fried and boiled they are used in soups, gumbos, and mix vegetables. Okra should be used while they are tender, once they start to harden, they are no longer good for cooking, and eating. We liked fried and boil okra. Boiled okra is good in field peas, and other green vegetables and soups.

Cantaloupe has yellow flesh and is sweet. Watermelon and cantaloupe are best when eaten fresh.

Some culinary uses: melon balls, and fruit salads. We mostly sliced our cucumber, sprinkle with salt, and ate them. Squash was another family favorite, we par boiled them first, sprinkle with salt, pepper, a little sugar, then fry with onions in lard.

Pomegranates, we raised them in our yard, you could sit down under a tree or on the porch, cut open the rind of a ripe pomegranates and eat them. You could swallow the seeds or reject them. Persimmon grew out on the terrain; we had a tree near the gully, and did not eat too many of them. We left them for the opossum to eat.

Nuts are different from fruits. We ate the seed of nuts and usually not the covering (shell). For example, peanut, we did not eat their covering we ate the seeds.

However, when we eat nuts, we eat the big seeds which are very expensive for the plant to make, as they are rich in oils, minerals, and vitamins. Pecan is good eaten right from the shell. Some culinary uses: peanut are commonly "roasted and salted" and are used much in baking. You will find them in breads, cakes, candy, cookies, ice cream and pecan pies. Pecan is a Southern member of the "hickory family." We had a few pecan trees in our yard, where I would sit down and eat them, fill up my pockets with pecans as I move around the farm. We also had a" black walnut" tree in our front yard. To eat them, we had to take a hammer or large rock to crack them open to get the meat, and they were very good.

Work on the farm was from "dawn to dusk." I did less work than anyone else, I was the water girl, and the youngest of the four children. I would go home during the day and draw fresh water from our well and take it back to the family working in the field. I watch very carefully when I went home alone. On the way back I would look for "snake drags" to see if any had cross my path while I was at home. Sometime I would see where a snake had cross my path while I was at home, I came to a complete stop and start running and sweating. I had a fear of snakes. At lunch time we all went home to eat. We kids played in the yard after we ate lunch. We used to bat bumble bees, play game of marbles, dodge ball, and yankee doodle. This is how we played yankee doodle game: we took a small stick, went under the house, stirred where we saw little mound of dirt, and sing as we stirred "yankee doodle your house is on fire" until the doodle come out. As I grew older, I relaxed on the front porch and read books at lunch time.

Sugar Cane.

Sugar cane is tall grass plant that grows in tropical and semitropical countries.

Sugar cane plants consist of sturdy stalks seven to thirty feet high. These stalks contain a large amount of sugar juice from which sugar, molasses also called syrup are made.

Sugar cane grows as tillers (shoots) from underground branches. The numerous stalks above the ground have no branches, but they have long, narrow leaves that are arranged .

In two rows. The sugar cane stalk is divided into several sections, like a bamboo cane.

These sections, which are called internodes, are connected by joints known as nodes. each "node" bears a bud, much like a "potato eye." The bud can be used to plant a new crop.

Most sugar cane is grown in regions where temperatures generally range between seventy five and eighty fahrenheit and where the rainfall is high. Sugar cane is grown chiefly from stem cuttings placed in furrows (narrow grooves) in the field and covered with soil. The bud on the nodes germinate into leafy shoots that emerges from the soil.

In a few weeks, the shoots produce stalks with nodes and internodes.

Most sugar cane is harvested from eight to twenty four months after planning. Uncle Alfedo and Rozell cut the cane by hand using a large steel knife like a machete.

The cut stalks are gathered into heaps, placed in the wagon and carried to the cane mill where we began the process of making syrup.

We made our own syrup from "sugar cane" at our own "cane mill." This was done by mule as they pulled a pole around and around to get juice from sugar cane where the stalks were fed into the cane mill and squeeze the juice into a large tub. When the tub became full, the juice taken to a big round boiler or vat. Fire was made under the vat to cook the sugar cane juice. As the juice cooked, we took the skimming of the top.

At times we drink cane juice before we started to cook it. It was very good.

The plummings from the squeeze cane stalks, was put on the ground for the mule to walk on.

This vat was located under a shelter, with only two sides closed in, the other sides were left open. The syrup was cooked and stirred until it was the right consistency (thickness) to be called syrup. When syrup was finish making, it was put into jars and some large containers, and ready to eat.

The whole family was involved in this process until it was completed. This was done once a year. Grandmother may have sold some of her syrup? She also, allowed other farmers to use her cane mill that did not have their own. She helped them in other ways, like small loans for farm supplies, seeds, and fertilizer, etc . . . .

We did not use tractors during our farming years to cultivate the farm land. We used plows pulled by mules and a few time, I remember Aunt Lillie plowed an oxen to help catch up the work that was behind. My uncle and brother plowed the fields, and they gave the "gee" and "haw" command to queen and nell, our mules.

Most farmers close around us were black farmers. Some of them were share croppers, other were owners, White farmers were near "Chances Store, and some were near Mount Andrews. Grandmother took us to Chances Country Store to get our school shots. A nurse would come there on certain days to give shots to school children. We were healthy children and was never sick. Although, we had our childhood diseases, like measle, chicken pox and the mumps. Aunt Lillie and aunt Freader had major operations to remove tumors, before they married and left home.

Grandmother cleaned us out occasionally, she gave us "castor oil" sometime I would gag on castor oil. Epson Salt and 666 were another bitter medicine we all hated it as well. Our grandmother and our aunts used to take "black draught" it was very bitter medicine too.

The white farmer, Mr. Cook ask grandmother, if she was caught up with her work? If so, would she help him pick "velvet beans" and he would pay us. So one day grandmother and the three of us girls went to Mr. Cook's farm to pick velvet beans; I scratched so much and then I started crying because those velvet beans sting me so bad. I worked to the end of the day, I did not go back the next day. I am not sure if any of us went back. Grandmother own her own field of velvet beans, they were black with little fur on them that itch you some terrible, once the fur get on your skin. We hated picking velvet beans, in our own field. I believed they were used to feed the hogs.

Farm management includes everything that farmers do to make farming profitable. To make a profit, farmer must sell their goods for more money than what It cost to produce them. Expert management helps lessen some of the financial risks of farming. Farmers have little or no control of risks caused by the weather, crops can be damage by heavy rain at planting or during the harvest season. A drought, floods, severe hail, or frost can destroy a crop at anytime. Sudden cold spell or violent storm can endanger livestock on ranges or in pastures. Hazard like these can wipe out an entire year's profit. Therefore, make efficient farm management. All the more important, an efficiently run farm should earn enough profit in most years to survive an occasional loss because of bad weather.

People Power. Off all things on the farm, you are the most valuable. Everything else allowed to break down, snap or perhaps have an off day, but you learn when to call it a day and finish a job tomorrow. Hands-on experience of working the land, not to manage other people. In working the land you will learn the feel of the wooden handle of a pitchfork, hoe, or spade. You will be surprise how you can become attached to your hand tools. Its human power, turning land, sowing seeds, working the crops, by hoeing, plowing and fertilizing. Skilled to handle livestock, milking the cows, feeding the pigs, helping calves to be born. Come harvest you reap the rewards for your efforts. In the 1930's the U.S. Government established programs designed to protect farms from the impact of surpluses. Measures were taken to prevent closure of farmers and the food shortage that might result. Therefore, minimum price were set by the government that farmers received for selected key farm products. It kept prices from falling below the minimum levels through "price support program."

Christmas. During Christmas time on the farm we had some exciting times. We decorated the "main" sitting/bedroom with hollies and the front porch. We believed in santa claus for a while. Mr. Simmons, our neighbor came to our house and talk to grandmother about santa claus is not coming this year, because he broke his leg. We believe him, not knowing he was not telling the truth. This tale upset us and we were disappointed about the sad news.

When grandmother went to town to buy candy, candy cane, oranges and other christmas goodies, she put them under the bed in bags in our bedroom. When Christmas Eve came she divided santa's goodies into four different shoe boxes. One box for each of us.

It did not take long for us to find out what was going on. We started looking under the bed and going through everything, without grandmother knowing it. When christmas came, we tried to act like we were so surprised at our gifts. Finally, she stop playing santa claus.

The weather there at that time of year was cold. I remember seeing snow in Alabama a few times, it was not a whole lot, but light sprinkles and snow flurry, it did not last long and soon melted. Parts of the state received snow. It rain quite a bit at times, and flooded in low lying areas.

During the spring of the year grandmother took all the beds down, boiled water, put some soap in it to scald down the bed railings and slats. The wooden and iron beds was wash down to deter bedbugs. The mattresses were put outside in the hot sun to help keep them fresh. As the rain fall during the summer months and storm comes up, it began to thunder and lightening close to us. I was very afraid, especially of lightening.

CHAPTER IV

Growing Up On The Farm

Growing up on the farm, we lived a normal life. It was kind of a safety net, we felt safe, no bills to pay, no rent, no worry about where our next meal would come from.

In the country we saw fewer people and saw them less frequently than you would see in the city. Even with wagon and a car, there is an element of isolation still in country life.

I could not have made this comparison while I lived in Mount Andrews, in the thirties and forties; but having gone away to a city where your livelihood depend on where you can find a job that pays enough to sustain yourself and family without being on some kinds of relief.

I really did not feel isolated on the farm because we kept busy during the week.

On the weekends, some work, but not as much, mostly chores around the house.

On Sundays, we went to church and met with other relatives and friends there. When we became school age we socialized with other school children, although we did not visit them at their homes often. We just saw them at either school or church.

Coming from Tuskegee at such an early age, into a new environment, I am sure the adjustment went well. I was too young to know the difference anyway.

When I became to know myself, I had blended in with the rest of the family. Neighbors were farther apart, so was shopping, schools, and churches, except Shiloh AME Church which was over the hill from where we lived.

Grandmother organized her trips to town usually on Saturday's. Clayton was about twelve or thirteen miles away from where we lived. Most times either Alfedo, or Rozell drove her in the wagon or car, after she purchase one. My sisters and I seldom went to Clayton, it was far and in between. Some positive things about living in the country was clean air, water, quiet and privacy. In addition to our "well," water we had a lots of fresh spring water around us. We drink fresh water and inhale fresh air, not to mention, the fresh vegetables and fruits we ate. I actually, got tired of eating field peas and turnip greens, because we ate so many of them. Today we go looking for fresh field peas, and turnips greens. I walked around and did some bird watching, listen to the birds singing throughout the day. It was truly fascinated to watch the hummingbirds as they flit from flower to flower in search of nectar. Someone has said, "a bird on the wing has found man looking up in envy, but a hummingbird by the feeder can stir up within him how awesome is his God."

Growing up on a farm was not a novelty it became routine chores. Weeding the garden, feeding the chicken, hogs, and mules to name a few. Although, farm routine was different from office routine. In daily farm chores, we were not disturbed by telephones and the clatter of machines.

An old farm adage says "early to bed and early to rise makes a man healthy, wealthy and wise." Our day began at dawn. We had to allow for dressing ourselves, making beds and eating breakfast. Then we go to work in the field until noon. At lunch time we went home to have our dinner. One of our aunts left the field in time to go home and cook lunch, which was a complete meal. After we ate, some of us took naps, or relaxed, some read. As children, most times we played games. After we wash dishes, the kitchen floor was swept and mopped when needed. I was not too adventurous in the kitchen. I did not do hardly any cooking while

I was with grandmother. After I got engaged to marry, then I started to cook more. I needed to know what I had to do when I left home. Most of the cooking was done by my aunts.

Evening came at the end of the day, we went home to have supper, and relaxed for awhile before bedtime. Everyday was not exactly the same pattern, some days we worked longer than other days. It depend on what we were trying to accomplished or finish. Sometimes we rode in the wagon to and from the field, most of the time we walk, depending on how far we had to go.

For breakfast we did not just eat breakfast food, as we do today. We ate fried chicken, fish, rice, eggs, bacon, stewed tomatoes and peaches, hot home made biscuits and flour bread, with home made butter that was made in our own churn. Grandmother and my aunts made homemade jelly and preserve from our fruit. It was a thrill, kind of like you were breaking some silly rule about foods we supposed to be eaten at each meal. We had mouthwatering breakfast and dinner. My aunts made the family favorite meals. We started the day with a good hearty breakfast that was needed to keep us until dinner time. Dinner is the meal we all love the most. It is the meal we remember the most from growing up and the meal we look forward to all day long. Dinner is the where you share good food and good feeling with your family. We did not eat fast food, TV dinners, we ate meals that created from scratch on the farm. We could smell the flavors and aromas of home cooking that say, "welcome home for dinner." The variety of boil, fried, stewed and baked food shared was heartwarming. One other thing I want forget, grandmother made very good lemon-aide. Nothing was like hoe cake corn bread, and flour bread that was cooked on top of the stove in a frying pan. Instead of pancake like today, we ate "flour bread" made from flour like biscuits.

Supper usually was left over food from dinner. Some vegetable and meats we had for dinner. Since, supper was at the end of the day, we did not have to rush in and eat, we could be more relaxed, because we did not have go back to the field. We had some chores like feed and water the dogs, cats, hogs, mules, and chicken, they all had to eat too. We helped clean up the kitchen, like warm water to wash dishes, and mop the floor.

Sometime we drew water from the well outside prior to cooking for cooking needs.

A fire had to be made in the wood stove before my aunts or grandmother could cook.

It took a little while for the stove to get hot. Once it got hot it cooked well. Depend on what you was cooking, or how long it take to cook, sometimes more wood had to be put in the stove for it to continue cooking. After relaxing for a while, we would prepare for bedtime. If it were cold weather, grandmother, my aunts, and us would sit around the fireplace discussing some issues prior to going to bed. We needed a good night rest to be ready for whatever farm task we had to do the next day. Farmers always rise at dawn and work all day long until dusk. They took water breaks, dinner and then supper which end the days work.

Grandmother used to get a local newspaper called "The Clayton Record," sometime she would read some of the newspaper at lunch if she had time, and finish it at night prior to going to bed. We usually had a full and busy day. As a child I played quite a bit in my spare time in the yard. Sometimes I went to the fruit trees around the house to get fresh fruit to eat. I very seldom got hungry, because there was so much to eat other than cooked food.

As children we had a few fights among ourselves. I remember one day while we were unloading dried corn from the wagon, Rozell and I got into an argument. I threw a hard ear of corn at him with all my strength, he ducked to keep it from hitting his head. Had the corn hit him he would been badly hurt. When my sisters and I had arguments, they use to call me "chicken legs," because my legs are thin. Of course, I used adjectives to describe them. Grandmother, did not hesitate to spare the rod on our backside, when needed. Sometimes she spared us from whipping, by giving us the LOOK, when we did something she did not like. She did not have to say anything. We knew what that meant. Stop doing what you are doing. I had got to the point, I would LOOK back, but I stopped what I was doing.

When grandmother whipped us, she pulled a small branch from a tree and pull all the leaves of it. She called that a switch. That what she whipped our legs, and backside with. She kept a plenty of switches in a corner of the room. I remember one day I was coming from school I was playing with a young boy, I believe his name was David Winsley, Jr., we were running across the field near the road where we normally walk. As we ran I was chasing him, I caught the brim of his hat as he continue to run that cause the brim of his hat to rip off. Once the brim ripped off, be became afraid that his father would be angry at him. He told his father when he got home, he was right his father was angry at him. The father came to our house that same night and told grandmother that I tore up his son hat. Even though we were just playing and it was an accident, grandmother whipped me for that anyway, because Mr. Winsley was angry about his son hat was destroyed. We walked from school everyday and to and from church on Sunday. One thing for sure, we got a plenty of exercise working on the farm and walking to and from church to church on Sunday.

We knew not to touch the switches. One of her favorite phrase, "I hate to keep whipping on you children, because you don't have a mother." Whenever she began to scold us, we could sing the chorus. One day while grandmother was giving me an "attitude adjustment" with one of her switches, I told her not to hit me anymore. I never apologized to her for saying that, but I wished I had. The four of us were raised in a christian home. Grandmother was strict on us. We looked forward to growing up and leaving home. I realized that we got the best training at home with her, even though she was strict. She made good people out all four of us. We grew up with respect for ourselves and other people; we learn what value mean. Grandmother was the only mother I remembered, strange that we never called her mother. We called her "grand ma" or grandmother. We all loved her very much. She use to let me sit on her lap and comb her long pretty hair. That was my quality time with her. I could get things from her that the other siblings could not get. Grandmother was an anchor in all our lives. She was the rock, the foundation on which we build our values and our lives.

We helped with farm work, and chores around the house, such as keeping the yard clean, pulled up weeds around the house, picked up the mail from the mail box about a half miles away, near Shiloh AME Church.

Woodpile. Wood was our fuel. Trees were sawed down and hauled home to be cut up. We had a pile of wood cut by my uncles and brother. After cutting the wood, they would stack it up into a big pile. We called it the wood pile. That where we took our load of wood in our arms and carried it to the kitchen for cooking or to the room where the fireplace to help keep us warm. We carried in firewood for the cook stove and fireplace. It used for cooking and we kept warm by the fire in the fireplace, from burning logs.

At night grandmother "banked" the fire in the fireplace so it would not go out during the night. She re-kindle it the next morning to bring it back up again. Sometimes the fire went out. I vividly remember seeing grandmother standing by the fireplace with her long dress pulled up in the back warming her backside. We laughed at her. I tried it a few times myself, it get pretty warm. Uncle Alfedo and Rozell was responsible for cutting the firewood. Grandmother and our aunts cooked on a wood stove. They made good meals, tea cakes, homemade cakes, and pies. Fried chicken fresh right off the yard.

They even kept the chicken feet, cleaned and fried them and made gravy, ate with hot homemade biscuits, butter, syrup or some preserves, were "good eating."

Homemade ice cream was made of milk, eggs, sugar, vanilla or lemon flavor, etc., they cooked the mixture and then put it in the ice cream maker, chunks of ice put in the ice-cream freezer, and hand crank the ice-cream machine until the ice-cream was thick enough to eat.

When the weather was not conducive to farming the women passes their time with quilting. This during the winter months, the adults did a variety of things, among them was making quilts. This project was done by using four cords suspended from the ceiling attached to four wooden rails with the dimension of a full size bed. The bottom of the quilt was attached to the rails, thin layers of cotton was spread over that layer, then the top of the quilt was hand stitched through the bottom. If the quilt was not finished by bedtime, it was rolled up with the chords, since it was located in front of the fireplace. When the hem was completed, and that was a finished product.

We were allowed to help with stitching. Being the youngest I slept with grandmother, when we first came there from Tuskegee. During the winter months she put so many quilts on the bed to keep us warm, it was hard for me to turn over in the bed. She had a"trundle bed" that Rozell, Ethel, and Doreather slept in. Later on my sisters slept in a regular bed in the side bedroom, and Rozell slept in the back bedroom with uncle Alfedo. As I grew, I started sleeping with my sister Doreather in the side bedroom.

I remember my grandmother and aunts washing clothes on a scrub board outside on a table in the backyard. We washed clothes at least once a week. I am not sure what day wash day fell on? It may have been on Friday? The back yard area was filled with clouds of steam and the smell of soap suds dripping from the clothes. The clothes were stirred with a laundry bat or stick. Grandmother made her own detergent call "lie soap" it was used on the clothes on the scrub board and on heavy stained clothes. She also bought large bars of soap for washing clothes and hands.

Scrubbing was to released the dirt prior to boiling. We used galvanized tubs to wash clothes, put them in a black iron wash pot to boiled the clothes. Fire was made under the black wash pot filled with water, to boil some of the clothes and bed sheets.

Water was drawn from the "well" for washing clothes on wash day. We carried water to the wash area where the wash tubs were on tables. After the labor of washing clothes they had to be rinsed, then water had to be squeezed from the clothès, prior to hanging clothes outside on the line to dry, when the clothes dried, we took them off the lines, they were ready for ironing. Then finally finishing by making the starch. She used a bottle with a sprinkler head on it and she had to iron clothes quickly. Ironing was a slow process in the days when iron had to be heated on a wood stove. We called it a "smoothing iron" was used to press the wrinkles out off clothes.

They complete the long day by pressing clothes, all the way down to sheets.

We also, took bath in a galvanized tub in the house, because we did not have a bathtub or sink.

We did not have to worry about expense of heating fuels, gas or electric cooking.

We used wood stove for cooking and fireplace for keeping warm. Kerosene lamps were used at night for light until we got electricity. I am not sure what year that was.

We went fishing a few times in streams, and creeks not to far away from home. My fishing were limited, because I was afraid to take the fish off the hook, once they were caught. Grandmother bought most our fish in Clayton at the fish market.

The fish I like most was "red snappers." Although, she bought mullets salted fish, etc . . . We would see minnows, tadpoles, and small turtles, during our fishing trip. We also, saw tadpoles and small turtles when went walking in the cow pasture where streams of water exist.

I was somewhat of a "tomboy" I climb trees in the hog pasture near the house like my brother did. I remember, one day as I was playing in the tree, I fell out off the tree right into a hog mud puddles. You can imagine what I look like.

On weekends, when some of our cousins came over to play, we went "gully jumping." One gully I did not make it across. I fell in and bruised my face and it was bleeding, and I started crying. I was following the older children. My brother got in trouble with grandmother, she gave him a whipping for letting me follow them in such dangerous places. Well, that ended the gully jumping for that weekend. When gully jumping, good judgment had to be applied. If part of the gully was to wide, go to a narrow part.

Since we did not have a radio in our home, we used to sit in the car and listen to the car radio. The only music we could get was "hillbillies," it sounded good. Today, we call it country western. We did not have television, or telephone. Tell a man or woman, would carry the message throughout the community. Sometimes we was informed on Sunday at church, if it was an important news.

We had a lots of fun with our cousins, as we played and communicated together. Uncle Alto Walker and wife, Expella, their *three younger sons were close to us. They were first cousins to my mother and aunts, and second cousin to us. They would not allow anyone to fight or pick on us when they were around. They stood their own ground. They were: Telonia, Alto Jr.,*Winsley, Robert, Melrose, we call him "cucu," we attended the same school and church. They also had a sister Leola, that lived at home, an older brother and sister that lived away from home, they lived in Detroit, Mich. I think they were by a previous marriage. Uncle Alto and family lived on the far side of Center Ridge Church, and we lived on the opposite side. Uncle Earnest Walker, grandfather's brother. He had quite a few children too. To name a few: Edie B, a tall girl with knock knees, Earnest Jr., we called his "sheep," May Bell, Brown, Cora, Algurtha, Hattie and Joe Walker. Edie B and Sheep was our school mates, we also attended Sunday school together. Wilson, Alto, and Earnest Walker were all brothers.

Our other cousins we played with that lived closest to us, were the Haslam twin girls, Thelma and Velma, we call them "bill and doll," there brother were: EJ, Seth, Calhoun, James and Jeff, Ozell and Cleo, and the two older sisters, Ophelia and RC. The Coxe's were also cousins lived close to us: Zera Lee, Myrtle Lee, John L., Rudolph and Curtis, three older sister Lula Pearl, Reasie Bell, and Ezella. The Simmon's were also cousins, they lived further down the road near Aunt Versey. The Simmons boys were: Robert, Ozell, Arthur, and Melvin, sisters: Lonnie Bell, Vinella, and Lula Mae. The Scovil's lived farther away over behind the backside of our farm, near our sugar cane and velvet bean field. The two girls, Verdell and Hattie Mae, I use to play with them. They had four brothers: Bobby, Haywood, Wilbert and Frank. Their two uncles were Tad and Winston, we call him "rabbit." Three other very good friends and school mates as well: Hullie, Evelyn and Grover Williams. Grover and I played together a lot. Evelyn was a close friend to my sister Ethel. James L and Jim R McNabb, was our neighbor, we use to make fun of the patches on their overalls, even though we played with them.

We did not have a playground, except at the schools. No parks were near by, we had large yards and open fields to play, run and jump. One of my favorite was skipping, as I made my way around. As time passed, grandmother allowed us to ride queen and nell our mules. So one day Doreather and I went on an odyssey to the far side of the farm behind where we lived, near the Scovil's Farm, to the sugar cane field. During our travel, I fell off queen as I talked to Doreather, looking back not paying any attention to where I was going. Queen walked under a tree with a low limb, just as I turned around, the limb caught me under my neck and queen just kept walking. I was pulled off, luckly I was not hurt, just a little shook up. Doreather and I laughed about it later. Queen, the larger mule the one I rode, was more calmer. Doreather rode nell, the smaller one, with more spunk. At times nell would start bucking and try to throw you off her back. The two of us made it back home safe.

I remembered once, grandmother went into town, either to sell or buy something. While she was gone, Uncle Alfedo help us to scramble eggs, we may have killed and fried a chicken? We had a feast eating, and made a conscientious effort to clean up everything before grandmother return. At other times when she went to Clayton, I put on my brother overall or pants to see how it feel. Grandmother did not allow us to wear pants. She said if God wanted us to be a boy, he would have made us one. I pulled off the pants before grandmother returned home.

As children, we never wanted for food and clothing. Aunt Lillie was a seam-stress, she made our work, school and church clothes. Our standard attire for work out doors, our dresses were made out of "juano"sack (fertilize sack), straw hat, and barefeet were ready for the farm to work with whatever was to be done that day. As the sun was coming up over the farm and the rolling fields, we were ready for the day.

Aunt Lillie also, made our church attire out of gingham and print dresses. When I was about twelve years old, grandmother started to buy us ready made dresses from town. Although, she tried to give me hand-me-down dresses from my sisters, since I was the youngest, but I threw a fit. So I got my new dress too.

Some of our cousins got jealous of how we dressed and said we thought we were better than them, because our grandmother was rich. I said, I do not know anything about that, and just looked at them. As I grew up, I was rather quiet and shy. Thelma Haslam said when I was small that I was selfish? I do not remember being selfish.

We visited occasionally with our cousins and played games. Once I fell asleep at the Haslam's house while grandmother and I was visiting. Mrs. Costella asked grandmother to let me stay the night and she will send me home that next morning. So I spent one night there and the next morning I went home.

Several of us walked from school together. We not only attended Center Ridge Church, along with our cousins and friends, we walked from Center Ridge Church to Shiloh AME Church, located near where we lived and attended service there. Not much excitement in those days for us, so we spent a lot of time in the church.

That's where I first met Haywood at Shiloh AME Church. At that time he was Methodist and I was Baptist. It took him sometime to make up his mind to come up to me and talk. Finally, he did Later on he started coming to the house, although he feared grandmother. During my courting days, if a boy wanted to marry a girl he had to ask her parents for her. As time passed finally, Haywood got to that point. He was quite uncomfortable asking grandmother for me. Once he got pass her, grandmother told him you have to ask her father too. Once he got up enough nerve, Haywood, then got Jamie Taylor, who had just married my oldest sister Ethel to go with him to Tuskegee to ask my father for me. Jamie teased him a bit, his knees was really knocking again. The three of us went to Tuskegee, and Haywood got the OK from both grandmother and my father to marry me. In the meantime, Rozell had already married. His first marriage was to Lu Versey Dorsey, in Mount Andrews, in 1942. from that union two sons were born: Robert and Arthur. That marriage did no work out. His second marriage was to Claudia Davis in the early 50's in Orlando, Florida. To this union they have six children: Rozell jr., his oldest son, died at age 8 years old with asthma. Then Herman, Loleta, Vera and Ernest, and Ernestine (twin). They all still live in Orlando today.

CHAPTER V

Country Critters

We had two dogs, Spot and Tan, and a few cats unnamed, mules, steers and bees. My brother and cousins did what they called "robbing the bee hives," to get honey. Bee hives were found in a hollowed tree look somewhat like a wasp nest. honey was in the honeycomb, and they drained the honey out into a container. A stick was wrapped with a piece of rag, then light it with a match and threw it into the hollowed tree to draw the bees out so they could get the honey.

Another popular play tool for young boys were: sling shot, pop guns, bb guns homemade bow-and-arrow, whistle made from reeds, and kites to fly and "race" one another to see who get to the finishing line first.

Bats roost on the barn, and wasp nest seem to be on all corners outside the house and cribs. In the woods we had raccoon, opossums, foxes, wild turkeys, bobcats, red head woodpeckers, buzzards, crows, hawks, mocking birds, robins, red birds, blue jay, sap suckers, and variety of other woodland critters. Summer evening, a whippoorwill sing from the treetop, late in the evening. Sound like they were singing "chip" fell off the white oak" repeatedly, and late at night owls hoot as they flew pass the house.

We used our mules and steers to pull the plows and cultivate the farmland. They are the most important and useful animal on the farm when it comes to cultivation.

They plow, pull the wagon, help in the process of making

syrup, ride them as you would ride a horse, to do errands. Mule and wagon were used to haul dead bodies to funeral service at church during our time.

During hunting seasons, Uncle Horace, Alfedo, and Rozell went hunting for such critters as: rabbits, squirrels, opossum, foxes and birds (doves and partridges), This also provided meat for the family. Once rabbits and squirrels caught, they were skinned then par boiled, season with red crushed pepper and to take out the wild taste.

After they got tender, my aunts would break them into pieces, flour them, and fry them in lard of fried meat grease until they were brown and crispy. Opossum was prepared the same way, although baked in the oven eat with sweet potatoes, that was good eating.

Hunting dogs were used to help them during hunting season. I had a problem with eating racoon, as soon as I found out it was racoon meat, I would spit it out. Guns were not strangers to us, even though we did not use them. Our uncles, and brother used them when hunting. Several shot guns both single and double barrel guns were kept on the gun rack in the house used for hunting. We call raccoon, coon most of the time.

My uncles and brother would go out at night with a lantern to hunt along with their dogs. The dog would pick up the scent of the track of raccoon, rabbits, squirrels, and opossum sometime they would run the coon up a tree, the dog would stand there and barked to until the hunters get there. Some dogs are fox dogs they run the foxes all night long trying to catch them. Foxes will catch your chicken right out of the chicken house and eat them, a hawk will fly down and catch your chicken too and eat them. A raccoon is a fighting animal, they will give a hunting dog a hard time. Bird dogs hunt for birds in the bushes and get them up to fly up, so the hunters will shoot at the birds.

Sometime men would do "turtle" hunting. They look for turtle around the water, sometime they come out on land and the hunters follow the tracks. They take a long pole and put an iron spear at the end, catch the turtle by sticking it with the spear in the water. Hunters do not hunt for buzzards, but they are unusual big black bird. They eat anything that dead. So don't lay down to long on the ground. They eat any dead animals. They eat their way through any thing dead. Crows and racoons will eat your corn right of the stalk.

You can see that farmers have great responsibility to protect crop. In vegetable garden, the farmer would make a "scare crow" to imitate a man, to keep the bird out off the vegetable garden.

CHAPTER VI

Economy and Politics

At the time we arrived in Mount Andrews, The Great Depression had just ended. Stock market crashed in 1929 and early 30's During my stay in Alabama, the two presidents that were in office during the time we were there were: Franklin D. Roosevelt, our 32nd; 1933-1945; and Harry S. Truman, 33rd President, 1945-1953.

President Franklin D. Roosevelt led the nation through the Great Depression, and World War II. Assuming the Presidency at the depth of the Great Depression, he helped the American people regain faith in themselves. He brought hope as the promised prompt, vigorous action, and asserted in his Inaugural Address, "the only thing we have to fear is fear itself."

He was elected President in November 1932, to the first of four terms. By March there were 13,000.00 unemployed, and almost every bank was closed. In his first "hundred days" he proposed, and Congress enacted, a sweeping program to bring recovery to business and agriculture, relief to the unemployed and to those in danger of loosing farms and homes, reform, especially through the establishment of the Tennessee Valley Authority. By 1935 the nation had achieve some measure of recovery, but businessmen and bankers were turning more and more against Roosevelt's New Deal Program. In 1936 he was re-elected by a top-heavy margin. Feeling he was armed with a popular mandate, he sought legislation to enlarge the Supreme Court, which had been invalidating key New Deal measures.

Roosevelt lost the Supreme Court battle, but a revolution in constitution law took place. Thereafter, the Government could legally regulate the economy. When the Japanese attacked Pearl Harbor on December 7, 1941, Roosevelt directed organization of the Nation's manpower and resources for global war.

During his presidency the Civilian Conservation Corps (CCC) an Emergency Conservation Work Act established March 31, 1933. CCC employed young men between the ages of 17-23 in work camps where they were assigned to various conservation projects. Enrollees were paid thirty dollar a month, twenty five dollars of which was sent home to the enrollee's families. From 1933 to 1942, over three million young men enrolled in the CCC, including 250,000 African American who were enrolled in nearly 150 all-black CCC companies. The enrollees, contributed to the protection, conservation, and development of the country's environmental resources. Enrollees planted trees, fought fires, and took part in pest eradication projects. They build and improved parks and recreation areas, constructed roads, build lookout tower and strung telephone and electric wires.

Money sent home by CCC enrollee assisted families hard hit by the depression. Their duties was divided by race, and often in presence of officially sanctioned racism. Black membership in the CCC was set at ten percent of the overall membership roughly proportional to the percentage of African Americans in the national population. However, because the economic conditions of blacks were disproportionately worse than those of the white, this race-based quota system did not adequately address the relief needs of African American Youth. This inhospitable environment was aided by the absence of a sustained commitment on the part of the Roosevelt Administration to end racist practices within the CCC.

It was my understanding that those who was in the CCC program had to qualify, it was the lower income farmer who did not have a farm of their own, and probable was share cropping. A lot of people had hard times during this period. There was a lot of talk at home about CCC and WPA (Public Works Administration). CCC and WPA were definite an issue during that time, but I did not connect to the economic conditions at that time. I learned that the WPA provided public work like constructions of buildings and schools. On May 6, 1935, the Work Progress Administration was created to help provide economic relief to the citizens of the United States who were suffering through The Great Depression.

I assumed it was to help the people especially, black, and the poor whites, who needed agriculture help so they could become more self-sufficient, and provide economic relief. I do not believe this effected grandmother in her agriculture endeavors. The Walker's farm seem to be booming while we were there, and very much alive. I do not remember Uncle Adolph living there at the time, but he came back to visit. Uncle Adolph and Uncle Alfedo were drafted in the Armed Services, during World War II. Uncle Adolph went into the Marines and Uncle Alfedo went into the Army I believe their length of time in service were two years?

One day The Department of War (now DOD), called grandmother about Adolph "missing in action" (MIA), he was on the front line fighting and had to get down into a fox hole. They thought he was dead. I remember grandmother crying, later she was notified that he made it out and was all right.

Uncle Alfedo Army Picture   Uncle Adolph Picture

From New Deal To Fair Deal.

When Harry S. Truman became 33rd President in 1945, he was a farmer, a businessman gone bankrupt, and unknown political from Missouri who suddenly found himself president. Of all the men who had held the highest office. Harry Truman was the least prepared. Having served as Roosevelt's Vice President for only three months. Truman now had to negotiate how to continue Roosevelt's New Deal policies with an increasing Conservative Congress. Truman's attempt to follow up on the "New Deal" with his own "Fair Deal" as America began to shift rightward politically, economically and psychologically. Two of his favorite phrases were:

> "The buck stops here" and "If you can't stand the heat, get out of the kitchen."

I am sure some farmers struggle to make ends meet, some had to do share cropping, because they did not have their own equipment nor funds to manage farming of their own. When farmers have the tools and training they need to feed themselves and their families, they gain the power and trust to withstand threats posed by poverty, disease, and war. In 1900, households relied primarily on local food productions from their farms. After his successful election campaign, Truman set out to prove that New Deal liberalism was not yet dead, proposing what he called the Fair Deal programs, in announcing the Fair Deal, said that the survival politics of New Deal with its dual policy of relief and reform were no longer what America needed.

Instead, the Fair Deal would redistribute income among people of various classes, transferring money from the very rich to the very poor. Truman's Fair Deal goals came down to six major initiatives: Civil Rights, Federal Housing Programs, Unemployment Insurance Benefits, new tax cut for the poor, Federal Funding for Education, and Federal Health Care and Health Insurance Program. The Fair Deal was largely a failure, in that few of these initiatives were made into law. His wife Bess never wanted Harry to be President. He grew to like the job. But after his second term and his failure to get his "Fair Deal" through Congress, he decided he would not seek re-election in 1952. When he return to Independence, crowds of thousand cheered him, one of their own who had risen to great heights and then come home.

It was my understanding that the Department of Agriculture would pay farmers to plant "kudzu." and "soybeans" to build up farm land, especially abandoned land. Therefore, federal policies must constantly evolve to promote stewardship in fight of new opportunities. Soybeans offeres the most exciting possibilities of all grains. The Soybean is extremely versatile, it's not only food for man and animal, but a vegetable that contain essential proteins we ordinary get only in high priced meats. Moreover, the soybean is also good "food" for the soil-a-green manure crop that returns as many soil nutrients. Soybean is one crop grower might be able to produce in competition with commercial, chemically grown soybeans.

CHAPTER VII

Religious Education, Inspirational

and Social Activities

"Not that I speak in respect of wants; for I have learned, in whatever state I am in this to be content. I know both how to be abased, and I know how to bound; everywhere and in all things I am instructed both to be full and to be hungry, both to abound and to suffer needs. I can do all things through Christ, who strengtheneth me" Philippians 4:11-13

The Walker Family attended Center Ridge Baptist Church, in Mount Andrews, Alabama. Our grandfather and grandmother were Deacon and Deaconess of this church.

The original Center Ridge Baptist Church, were torn down after we left Mount Andrews, and rebuilt a much smaller church. We were in church from babies. I use to watch grandmother make bread and wine for Communion Sunday. She made up her own bread from scratch, without putting baking powder in it, to keep it flat. She would take the rolling pin and roll it out thin and cut it into small squares. She made the grape juice and used it for wine.

At Center Ridge, when we were growing up, the preacher did not preach every Sunday. He preached one Sunday out of a month, on the Third Sunday. We had Sunday School every Sunday. I understand they have service there now twice a months?

Center Ridge Baptist Church as it Stand Today

Once a year during the summer months, the Ladies Aid's and Eastern Starr and others celebrated with a lots of good southern food right on the church ground, after service on that Sunday. Tables were set up in front of the church all over the yard, where each family would bring their cooked food and place it on the table. We went from table to table to sample the delicious food. There were so much food, you never seen anything like it. They had a variety of southern cooked food, home made pies and cakes, fried chicken, potato salad, cooked fresh vegetables, I just can not name it all. Then came time for clean up, everyone had to clean up around their table and leave the church yard the way they found it.

I confessed Christ at the age of 15, during our annual "revival." I sat on the "mourners" bench for seven years, trying to get converted. I made up my mind that I will not follow anyone up front. I had to feel something for myself. Finally, one Friday night as the preacher had us to stand and he extended an invitation to accept Christ. I was crying very hard something struck me, and I fell on the chair out in front of me so hard, I broke the chair down completely. Later, someone in the church put the chair in the choir loft for a while, before destroying it. I was baptized in Center Ridge Church pool down in the woods, not far from the church. We marched pass the cemetery down in the wood to a nice pool the church had built, along with a small house for changing clothes.

My brother and sisters joined the church much earlier than I did. During revival times, before I was converted, I prayed and cried a lot. I went away from the house into the field, so I would not be disturbed while I prayed. After I met Haywood, I prayed harder, because I did not need him on my mind, I need Jesus to bring me through this. Our church had a summer revival every year. I enjoyed hearing the choir sing, even though they sang ""acappella." I always did congregational singing. Doreather and I use to sing at home.

Grandmother told us that we had melodious voices. There is something about live singing and that provided special inspiration for the moment. Perhaps singing in the church can help us face the task ahead, disappointment, frustration, and pain. There is a message in songs. An old familiar hymn like "A Charge to keep I have, a God To glorify," and "come ye that love the Lord . . . " All deacons know and sing these old hymns. These hymn reminds us that we are not alone, we can rest safely in our Saviors care. Our mother sing in the choir. Our father was a trustee at Saint Mark Missionary Baptist Church in Tuskegee, Alabama.

Some of My Favorite Songs: Blessed Assurance, What a Friend we have in Jesus, Nearer, My God to Thee, Holy, Holy, Holy . . . just to name a few. The black church during our time, choirs and the congregation sing without music. Their songs deals with how black people see God, the world, and themselves from the vantage point of the oppressed.

> "I have indeed seen the misery of my people in Egypt. I have heard them crying out because of their slave drivers, and I am concerned about their suffering. I have come down to rescue them . . ."
>
> (Exodus 3:7-8).

Baptist churches was not members of local associations, no department of Christian education to provide a needed service, like workshops, lectures, classes to educate church leaders in this important area of ministry like today's churches. But I am sure they did the best that they could with what they had. Black music comments on the history of that pilgrimage; a journey of sorrow, joy, despair, hope, frustration and fulfillment.

To a large extent the power of sermon is determined by how well the black preacher can "sing" the sermon. Many black preacher during those days did a lot of hoopla, more social preaching, rather than coming from the bible. This is not to suggest that black congregation do not value preparation, both academic and spiritual, and the content of the sermon. The black preacher must preach to the needs of the people.

To a large extent, a black church is judged by its spiritual tone, many members become emotional and shout during preaching and singing. Some just move their head or pat their feet. The spirit does not affect each individual in the same manner. The people of God have always been a singing people whose experience shaped their songs.

> "Make a joyful noise unto the Lord, all ye lands, Serve the Lord with gladness; come before his presence with singing."
>
> Psalm 100:1-2

The churches in our area had their own cemeteries, located either in front, side or back of the church; unlike today's churches. During the early thirties when a member or person deceased, they were not embalmed, when people died they laid them out on the bed, wash them and put clothes on the body. Put them in a wooden box. The "wake" was at home the night before the funeral the next day. They sat up all night long at the wake, relative and friends would come to the house during wake to view the body. It was then taken to church the next day in a wagon pulled by mules. Only those who could afford a casket and a hearse use them.

Our church had good cool fresh spring water. Located down the hill from the church, surrounded by woods. As I mention earlier, the original Center Ridge Church was a much larger church, before re-building it. It has loss it's "identity" as we remember it when we were growing up.

The deacons sat to the left front of the church called "the Amen's corner." Across from the right facing the deacon, sat the deaconess. The "mourners bench" was the first two benches in the center isle of the church. There were isles on each side of the center isle, from right to left with benches (pews). There were an extension with benches in the back of the center isle separated from the center seats by walk way or hall parishioner use to go to and from the church. Every church have a family or deacon that are in control of the church. Uncle Alto Walker was the head during our time. Today the Guice's are the leaders. Gilbert and Minnie B. Guice are still alive and there at Center Ridge Baptist Church. They are some mighty fine people.

While in Sunday School, we learned bible verses, at times we had to recite them. Sunday School Teacher would give us poems to learn prior to Easter to recite on Easter Sunday. I was stage fright, and every time I had to recite a poem, I got emotional at the end before I sat down. It took me a long time to get over that. When we dressed on Sundays, we wore ribbons in our hair or hat with a streamer running down the back.

Me and Doreather in hats, much older here

It was customary for church family to invite the preacher to their home for dinner, after service, some Sunday's. When the preacher came to grandmother's house, we were not allowed to eat at the table while the preacher ate. We had to wait until he finished eating, then we could eat. I use to crack the door a little to peep in, to see if any food was left. I thought the preacher would eat all the fried chicken. Preacher's could put away some food.

In spite of the country life, we had some fun. On May 28th of each year, the community leaders at Mount Siller gave an outing it was held on Mount Siller Baptist Church ground. They barbequed a whole pig and made "brunswick stew" that was very delicious.

There was a band and plenty of good food to eat, and the people had a good time. The few times we went there usually they have a large crowd.

Now that I am older and wiser, help to show how the season of life offer you opportunities to grow in Christ, body, mind and soul. I am just highlighting some nuggets of wisdom from past years. Now time can bring you gentleness, maturity and a greater usefulness for God.

There may be times our spiritual leaders are not what they should be. When leader fail, whether it unintentional sin or open defiance, it easy to become discourage or disillusioned. But it's a double tragedy if we become cynical and turn away from God because of them. We must remain faithful and focus on God. Other may prove untrue, but Jesus never fail. "He is the same yesterday, today, and forever. Hebrews 13:8

Remember, there are many ways to worship God, but only one God to worship. We must continue to pray without ceasing, that is we must always be in a state of readiness to pray, whether on our knees, riding along in our car, walking, sitting at home or even in the church. God is always there for us.

Even back in those days, all people did not worship God. Some came to church and never went in side, especially some of the men, they hung around on the outside and communicated, some brought liquor and got intoxicated down by the church spring which was down the hill from the church. I heard a big fight started. This was probably where moonshine liquor was made not too far away and someone would come there to sell it to those who hung around the outside of the church? The devil is busy at all times and everywhere. This was not every Sunday, I remember only one incident. They probably was not church members. Teenage boys would go to different churches to meet girls. They were not interested in the church service, they looking for a decent girl to date.

CHAPTER VIII

Uncles and Aunts That Lived Away From Home

Uncle Horace, his wife Annie Bell, and the children lived near Clayton, about Ten miles from us. They lived in the family farm house. To this union were nine children:

Elodies, Horace, Jr., James, UL, Herbert, Develma, Annie Glory, Wilson and Gladys Walker. Uncle Horace had a large farm, included: Live stocks, herds of cattle, hogs, and poultry, that the family managed very well. He also, had his own equipment to cultivate his farm. He used mules and tractors. Uncle Horace, served in the United State Army during World War I.

Uncle Horace and Aunt Annie Bell family house are still there. The children manage it, especially, James Walker, their son that moved back there from Detroit, Michigan several years ago. He and wife Evelyn, had a prefabricated home put together across the road from the family farm house. He managed his deceased parent property, and when the Walker family return to visit or just want to get away, they stay in the family house.

Aunt Armiller, lived over behind Uncle Horace's house just past Elam Church alone with her husband, Ervin. They lived in the family farm house, along with their eight children: Coliage, Essie Mae, Ann Esther, Velma Ree, Verdell, Bob, Ruth and Erwin, Jr. They attended to their farm, and raised livestock, poultry, hogs cows, chickens . . . but on a somewhat smaller scale than grandmother and uncle Horace. Their oldest son, Coliage, was killed in a truck accident near Clayton. The county was doing work on the road during the day. They left at the end of their work day, and left a huge pile of dirt in the middle of the road. Without any road signs, indicating work ahead, no lights or reflector at night. When this accident happen, Coliage was thrown off the truck between the wheels and the truck ran over him; something like that? When grandmother got the news she started crying, and so did we. My sisters and I were so afraid of the dead, we all slept in the same bed that night, with the cover pulled over our heads.

Aunt Armiller

We were close to Uncle Horace and Aunt Armiller and we visited often. I remember one Sunday grandmother took us to Aunt Armiller house to dinner with her and family. I thought she and Aunt Annie Bell was the best cooks in the world. They both were excellent cook and you could literally hurt self eating. Well, at Aunt Armiller, that Sunday I made a pig out off myself, I ate so much, after leaving the table, I went in one of her bedrooms, got on the floor and rolled from side to side. I did not eat that way again. Even though they baked cakes, pies, cobblers, southern fried chicken, they prepared very tasty meals. Their southern fried chicken was out off this world. Chicken just do not have the same taste today. Velma Ree and Doreather was close cousin and Verdell and I was close.

Aunt Ethel and husband Neal, we called him by his last name. They lived in Union Springs, Alabama. I believe they farm somewhat on a much smaller scale. They had three children: Dorothy, Denver, and Jaunita. They use to visit grandmother when they could. Aunt Ethel always got sick from riding in the car from Union Springs to grandmother house in Mount Andrews. She started throwing up, sometime they had to stop on the side of the road. Other times she made it to grandmother's house, but was still sick.

Aunt Alve

Aunt Alve marrid to Edmund Haggins, and moved to Tuskegee. From this union five children were born: Mary Alice, Iwilda, John, Brenda and Shirley. Alve met Mr. Haggins through our daddy. He was the person who drove our daddy down from Tuskegee to Mount Andrews to visit us. We went to visit Alve in Tuskegee from time to time. Her first baby son, sudden died at six months old. I thought he was the prettiest baby I had ever seen. It must have been crib death? They had a vegetable garden, no farm. Aunt Alve remarried after Mr. Haggins died, to a man last name was Thompson. No children to this union. They operated a "cafe" and served southern style food.

Aunt Lillie lived in Birmingham, Alabama with her husband Sam. No farm, no children. I went to visit Aunt Lillie in Birmingham after grandmother moved there with her. Aunt Freader, lived with her husband, Charles Stevenson in Commer, not far from Mount Siller Church. Lite gardening, no children We visited occasionally.

Aunt Larcenia

Aunt Larcenia along with husband, Glen lived in East Chicago, Indiana. One child Ernestine. They had a vegetable garden. Her husband Bama we called him, he worked at one of the mills there in Indiana? Aunt Larcenis' husband last name was Walker too. That made her Larcenia Walker Walker. Before Larcena married Bama, she was stood up by Kid Jones "groom" to be. In an attempt for her first marriage. Quite a few relatives and friends were invited to the wedding. Our front yard were filled with people. The ceremony was to take place on the front porch of grandmother house. After a long wait, the groom did not show up, I suppose he got cold feet, Finally, the invited guests went home. I thought that was very embarrassing to our family.

Aunts: Lillie, Freader and Larcenia, and Alve, were still living at home when we move there. They married late in life, like early or late 40's.

Uncle Adolph, left home early in life, he also lived in Birmingham. For awhile, no children. Later on children born out off wedlock by some lady he was living with, later on in life he married her. Therefore, the children does not carry the Walker's name.

Even though the siblings lived away from home, as farmers, had the same work schedule they too work from "dawn to dusk." Uncle Alfedo, never married. It was hard to marry a Walker.

I remember going over to stay with Uncle Horace and Aunt Annie Bell for a week to visit and play with their daughter "Little Annie." That what we called her at that time. While I was there, I played with Little Annie and Dorcus Grubbs. Dorcus was one of the prettiest black girl I had ever seen. Her father was a "mulatto." She was dark skin, but her hair was straight and black. While I stayed at Uncle Horace during my visit, Wilson, their son was about nine months old. One day I holding the baby and dropped him. Aunt Annie Bell shouted at me for dropping the baby, he wiggled right out off my arms. So I did not hold the baby anymore while I was there.

Later on, Little Annie came to visit grandmother for a week to play with me. We had a good time that week

Aunt Versey

Aunt Versey, and husband Otis lived on a rock hill with their children. They lived about two miles down the road from us. To this union seven children were born: George W., James E., Otis, Jr., Ernest, Versey Mae, Mary and Cobb Wilson(CW) Gamble. They lived the closest to us, that cause us to visit one another more often.

As a matter of fact, Doreather baby sit George, and I baby sit James. I stayed with Aunt Versey for quite a while to baby sit, while they worked their farm. She raised baby chicks, she had a incubator to hatch baby chicks. When I say rocky ground, I mean big rocks, you had to be careful walking around on the outside. Many toes were stumped. While stayed there baby sitting, I played with two children Otis mother and father raised their grandchildren, Mamie and Theotis Rogers. We call him "fee" I visited them sometime when I was not too busy baby sitting. They did not live far from Aunt Versey.

We were all right there together. One of my other duties in addition to baby sitting, I carried water to Otis and Aunt Versey while they worked in the field. I put the baby on my hip and a big jar of water in my hand and took it to the field to quench their thirst.

Sometime after grandmother bought a new car, I did not want to baby sit anymore. One day I left aunt Versey's house and walked all the way back to grandmother, which was about two miles by myself. I told her that I did not want to baby sit anymore, she said I did not have to, if I did not want to; so she did not send me back to Aunt Versey's house.

While baby sitting for Aunt Versey, I did some childish things. I remember, once I took some of Otis, "snuff" he use to dip, when they were not at home. I wanted to see what it taste like, well it made me dizzy. During my conversation with Aunt Versey, told me she wanted me to learn how to kill a chicken, or maybe I asked her how to kill a chicken. So, one day I tried to wring a chicken's neck like I saw her and my other aunts do. There were not enough strength in my hand or wrist to wring a chicken neck. Therefore, I could not do it. I tried but the chicken got away. I went inside the kitchen and boiled a kettle of hot water, and I went back looking for the same chicken and found it. This time I open the chicken mouth and poured hot water down its throat; The chicken ran away from me again, and went under the crib. I became very scared that the chicken would die from what I did. I just remember the outcome of the chicken incident, but I never did that again. When grandmother and my aunts killed chicken they would approach their unlucky prey and swoop, down came her hand, wrapped around the chicken's neck. With a twist of her wrist, dinner was ready to be place in the hot water to take off the feathers. The chicken lay naked and ready to be floured. Its feathers soon to be the stuffing for a pillow.

In 1941 grandmother bought a brand new Ford Car, and paid for it cash. It was very flashy and fancy car. Uncle Alfedo and Rozell were the drivers to take her where she wanted to go. Also, Alfedo drove around to check out the girls. Some Saturdays Rozell took grandmother to Clayton in the wagon and or car for her to sell

fresh eggs, at the farmer's market. After Alfedo and Rozell left for
Central Florida to live, Doreather learned how to drive and drove
some for grandmother.

Southern dialect spoken by Southerners. I listen to my
grandmother and aunts use Southern dialect during our time there.
Their pronunciation of words were short and choppy, and their
words were cut short. Let me share with a few examples: "chillon
for children, saddy for Saturday, gwine for going, git for get, yistidy
for yesterday, haint for ghost, den for then, dem for them, naw for
no." We picked up this way of speaking. But we learn better when
we grew older, and attended school.

I began to use the dictionary to look up unfamiliar words that
I heard, but some of these words were not found in the dictionary.
Southern people spoke in their vernacular. They have a long
southern drawl, and it hard to get rid of it. Sometime when people
leave one environment to another environment, for example, people
leave the south and move north, they have a tendency to pick up
the northern accent. So environment plays a great part on how we
speak and how we explain ourselves, not to mention education
plays a great part in self-expression.

Closing my eyes I can see a vision of grandmother making a
fire in the fireplace where we sat around and talked or relaxed.
Sometimes we roasted sweet potatoes in ashes in the fireplace. They
were good and we had lots of fun. Grandmother was tall, slim, fair
skin, good looking and smart business woman. During the week
she wore a straw hat to keep the sun out off her face. I did not
remember grandfather, he was a farmer too. Dark skin and full of
fun. He died of a heart attack. Growing up in this environment
has made me humble and grateful for having spanned from a rural
setting to the information age.

CHAPTER IX

Back In The Fall Of Our lives.

"There are obviously two educations.
One should teach us how to make a living
And the other how to live."

—James Truslow Adams

Education.

Schools during our time, we were not integrated. Blacks and whites went to separate schools. Also, teacher were allowed to whip children for causing problems: fighting, talking back, talking out in class or when children kept getting out off line during lineup. I remember, once during line up, I was out off line talking, the principal came over and whacked me across my back with a switch and said "I told you to stay in line." Well I stayed in line.

Rozell, Ethel, Doreather, and myself went to Center Ridge Public School. I started at an early age, before school age. My brother and sisters took me to school along with them. They could not leave me home alone, so I went to school with them. I sat in the corner, but I listen and began to learn. We walked about two miles one way to school each day. Sometime I would ride my brother's back part of the way to and from school. For a couple of years my sisters and I made perfect attendance and was given a dress a piece. At some point in grammar school, I made two grades in one year.

I was promoted at the end of the year in December, and again at the end of the school year in May. One of my problems was arithmetic. My emotions ran high as I sat in class waiting to be called on to go to the "blackboard" to solve a problem. My older sister Ethel helped me with math at home. She was very good in mathematic. While attending Center Ridge High School, we were taught by two preachers. Reverend O.L. Gamble, was my eight grade teacher. I was a straight A student in his spelling class. Reverend G. H. Cossey, was my eleventh grade teacher.

My School Days

Schools in those days, teacher's had more control over students, because of the whipping that was allowed. You did not have the violence and unrest like today's school children. I remember one incident happen while we were in Center Ridge High School. James L. McNabb had it out with the teacher. It was right after lunch, when we returned to class. He probably was talking in class and the teacher asked him to stop talking. James L. gave the teacher a smart remark, and the teacher hit him with a switch. All hell broke loose at that point, James and brother Jim R started throwing books at the teacher. Then half of the class chimed in throwing books. I stood up and tried to stop them, shouting "stop it." "stop it." The end results, James and his brother got suspended from school.

I remember when we were in grammar school, we had to learn, write and recite our "times tables: starting from one through twelve Samples of 1, 2, 3, & 12

1x1=1	2x1=2	3x1=3	4x1=4	12x1=12
1x2=2	2x2=4	3x2=6	4x2=8	12x2=24
1x3=3	2x3=6	3x3=9	4x3=12	12x3=36
1x4=4	2x4=8	3x4=12	4x4=16	12x4=48
1x5=5	2x5=10	3x5=15	4x5=20	12x5=60
1x6=6	2x6=12	3x6=18	4x6=24	12x6=72
1x7=7	2x7=14	3x7=21	4x7=28	12x7=84
1x8=8	2x8=16	3x8=24	4x8=32	12x8=96
1x9=9	2x9=18	3x9=27	4x9=36	12x9=108
1x10=10	2x10=20	3x10=30	4x10=40	12x10=120
1x11=11	2x11=22	3x11=33	4x11=44	12x11=132
1x12=12	2x12=24	3x12=36	4x12=48	12x12=144

We also, had to memorize and recite each county in the state of Alabama. As well as the capitol of each State in the United States. I also, remember our school visiting Rosenwald Elementary School in Clayton.

We went there for a field day exercises where we did acrobatic stunts. Our girls made a pyramids with students, they build up from the ground, students stacked on top of each other. The last student stood on the very top of the pyramid. When we completed, each student would jump off. Like something you see in a circus. Our students were uniformed with blue outfits called "bloomers." Center Ridge School girls competed with the girls at Rosenwald School.

Mrs. Taylor, elementary teacher used to punish her pupil by pinching them with her broke off thumb and make you sit under a small table. One day she pinched me with that thumb and sat me under that small table. I cried and screamed so loud like she was killing me, until she told me to come from under the table. She told grandmother what I did. Grandmother chastise me for that later.

When I got to the 10th grade, I caught up with my two sisters Ethel and Doreather, the three of us was in the 10th grade at the same time. Rozell stayed out of school more than we did because he had to help on the farm with plowing. Farming did not keep me and my sisters out off school. There in the 10th grade the principle kept the whole class back. I am not sure how he got away with that. I think that's how I caught up with my sisters.

In high school we did not follow a particular discipline, we studied most everything offered, including successful farming, everyday foods, and modern clothing. In 1930's and 40's as the farm population shrank and agricultural emphasis decreased in school books and educational materials, educators focused on agriculture as an occupational specialty, rather than an integral part of every student's life. Agriculture education was mainly offered to those few students wanting to make a career of agriculture.

I played basketball in high school as a "forward." Once, our school visited Commer High School to play against their girls. They were beating the socks off Center Ridge, the coach pulled me off the side line, I went in and made a centerline shot (goal), Those were the only two points our school made that day. Center Ridge screamed and cheered as if we had won the game. Today Center Ridge School is torn down. Students now go to the School in Clayton, Alabama

In our literature class, we studied about and wrote papers on the lives of such great men as: Oliver Wendell Holmes, Ernest

Hemingway, Shakespeare, Alfred Lloyd Tennyson, Henry Wadsworth Longfellow, just to name a few. Two favorite poem That I liked, "The House By The Side of The Road." And "Psalm of Life." Literature, is A body of writings in prose or verse. It is imaginative, and creative writing. Listen to the words carefully as you read these two poems.

The House By The Side Of The Road

Sam Walter Foss

There are hermit souls that live withdrawn
In the place of their self-content
There are souls like stars, that dwell apart,
In a fellowless firmament;
There are pioneer souls that blaze their paths
Where highways never ran—
But let me live by the side of the road
And be a friend to man.

Let me live in a house by the side of the road,
Where the race of men go by—
The men who are good and the men who are bad,
As good and as bad as I
I would not sit in the scorner's seat,
Or hurl the cynic's ban—
Let me live in a house by the side of the road
And be a friend to man.

I see from my house by the side of the road,
By the side of the highway of life.
The men who press with the ardor of hope,
The men who are faint with the strife.
But I turn not way from their smiles nor their tears,
Both parts of an infinite plan—
Let me live in a house by the side of the road
And be a friend to man.

I know there brook-gladdened meadows ahead
And mountains of wearisome heights;
That the road passes on through the long afternoon
And stretches away to the night.
But still I rejoice when the travelers rejoice,
And weep with the strangers that moan.
Nor live in my house by the side of the road
Like a man who dwell alone.

Let me live in my house by the side of the road—
It's here the race of men go by.
They are good, they are bad, they are weak, they
are strong,
Wise, foolish—so am I;
Then why should I sit in the scorner's seat,
Or hurl the cynic's ban?
Let me live in my house by the side of the road
And be a friend to man.

We learned language of literature: prose, poetry, short story, sonnet, iambic, lyric, and epic. As you read my second favorite poem, listen to the lyric, expressing personal emotions, . . . " Life is real! Life is earnest! . . . we must "learn to labor and to wait."

A Psalm Of Life

Henry Wadsworth Longfellow

Tell me not, in mournful numbers,
Life is but an empty dream!-
For the soul is dead that slumbers,
And things are not what they seem.

Life is real! Life is earnest!
And grave is not its goal,
Dust thou art, to dust returnest.
Was not spoken of the soul

Not enjoyment, and not sorrow,
Is our destined end or way;
But to act, that each tomorrow
Find us farther than today.

Art is long, and Time is fleeting,
And our hearts, though stout and brave,
Still, like muffled drums, are beating
Funeral marches to the grave.

In the World's broad field of battle,
In the bivouac of life,
Be not lime dumb, drive cattle!
Be a hero in the strife!

Trust no Future, howev'er pleasant!
Let the dead Past bury its dead!
Act,—act in the living Present!
Heart within, and God O'erhead!

Lives of great men all remind us
We can make our lives sublime.
And, departing, leave behind us
Footprints on the sands of time.

Footprints, that perhaps another,
Sailing o'er life's solemn main.
A forelorn and shipwrecked brother,
Seeing, shall take heart again.

**Let us then be up and doing,
With a hear for any fate;
Still achieving, still pursuing,
Learn to labor and to wait.**

Another one of my favorite is Learning. Leaning is ongoing, one never stop learning. "learning is wealth to the poor, an honor to the rich, and aid to the young, and support and comfort to the aged." There are three classes of people in the world: The first learn from their own experience—these are wise, the second learn from the experiences of others—These are the happy, and the third neither learn from their own experience nor the experience of others—these are fools,"

Imagine being able to do anything you wanted to do without having to be concerned about cost or consequences. You could have success without risk or sacrifice, education without exams. We realize, though, that's not the way life works. To know the joy of success we must pay the price of commitment, study hard and learn from our failures.

One of our high school teacher, I believe he was Professor Blount, often told us to "think before you speak." That is true even of today; sometimes we blurt out the wrong thing or it comes out the wrong way during our conversation. Another one of his "saying" "he who has never made a mistake, have never done anything, he that make too many want do much." That tells us none of us are perfect. We are human and we are prone to make mistakes. So we have to be careful in what we say, do and think. Especially, what we say and do, of course saying indicates what were are thinking, at least some of what we think.

I started learning at an early age. As a child I was very inquisitive, and asked questions about many things that I did not understand. I enjoyed finding out information on my own as well.

Ethel got married while in the 12th grade, to Jamie Taylor from Mount Siller, April 24, 1948; and completed high school in

Barber County Training School in Clayton, AL. After their first child Arnold was born, they moved to Gary, Indiana. They lived in Gary for many years. To this union three children were born: Arnold, Esther and Kelvin. Ethel deceased, March 29, 1974 with cancer. Jamie deceased about six month to a year after Ethel death. I also, married while I was in the 12th grade, I just had turn 18 years old to Haywood Eutsey, Jr., December 28, 1948. Haywood was from Clayton. We dated and wrote letters to each other for over two years. When Haywood and I got married we cross Alabama line to the State of Georgia, in Georgetown, Georgia to a Justice of Peace and married there. My Aunt Freader and Haywood's Uncle Cleveland were our two witnesses. Cleveland was home on a furlough from the U.S. Army, The reason we went to Georgetown, to get married, Haywood and I had taken our blood test, and it was late coming back. He said he had to get back to Florida to his "fruit picking" job and he did not want to wait. After marriage, we stayed one night with Haywood's Grand mother and father Minnie and David Young in Clayton. We left the next morning by greyhound bus for Haynes City, Florida, in Polk County.

Doreather was the only one of us, graduated from Center Ridge High School and not married. She married sometime after graduation to Reverend James McNabb, April 5, 1951, a "home boy." He had been a preacher from his youth. They stayed in Mount Andrews for a while, then moved to Atlanta, Georgia, James did a few years with the U. S. Army. They later moved to Gary, Indiana. They lived there several years and raised their two children: Lewis and Linda. In the early 90's the McNabb family moved to Stone Mountain, Georgia, where they now live today. Rozell did not graduate from High School he dropped out off school in the 9th grade.

Ethel and I did not have to get married, we thought we were in love, and could not wait. I was a virgin when I married, and I believe my sisters were too. Pregnancy in those days by young girls were not as prevalent as it is today. A few girls did get pregnant. Grandmother wanted to know "while I did not wait until I graduated, before I got married." I told her that I planned to continue school, since I was already in the 12th Grade. I kept my promise to grandmother that I would stay in school and graduate, so did my sister Ethel.

After Haywood and I arrived in Florida, I transferred from Center Ridge High School to Oakland High School in Haynes City, and started to school in January 1949, and studied for six months, and graduated June 1949.

Oakland High School

Haywood and I stayed on Avenue J in Haynes City, in a little three room house, that he had rented from Johnny and Trudy Ware. The house was located on their property next to their house, near the railroad tracks. I walked to school everyday, while Haywood went to work. I studied my school assignments and some days I would go to Mrs. Ware's house and sit in her orange tree and eat oranges. I had never seen an orange tree before. Mrs. Ware said "eat all you want but, do not make yourself sick."

Me and Haywood After Marriage in FL

I think God for giving us a mind that are capable of learning and blessed our world with schools, where minds are shaped and broadened. Schools in our time were more of a safe haven for students. Students must used their ability to study, absorb, and apply their learning in whatever aspect of life that confronts them.

Haywood left Florida when fruit picking season was over and went to Hightstown, New Jersey where his father lived. I stayed in

Haynes City until June and graduated. Most night I stayed at Mr. And Mrs. Ware's during Haywood absence.

My Graduation Picture

After graduation, I left by greyhound bus for Highstown, New Jersey to join Haywood Jr. In Mount Andrews today, if you go there you would not see any farming. There is not much to see. Mount Andrews is now defunct. The mail routes for Mount Andrews have been divided between Midway and Clayton, Alabama. The young people we grew up with, most of them have migrated north, while other moved away to other part of the country. The older people that stayed either died or not farming. Farming came to a stop. I guess they live on Social Security.

What use to be the Walker's Farm, is now grown up with bushes and trees. It has loss its identity and very hard to recognize as how it looked when we live there. A few homes there are far and in between, especially, in the area where grandmother's farm was. Center Ridge Baptist Church is still there, but are much smaller than the original church. Shiloh AME Church is still there and look the same.

After Grandmother dissolved the farm, the animals were taken to Uncle Horace's farm. Mules, cows, steers, chicken, the one they could catch. Some chicken were left there and was laying eggs, but they would not hatched, because the roosters were not around. Grandmother had a hired hand, after we left to help her on the farm, as well as some of aunt Versey's children.

Grandmother became ill, and later moved to Birmingham to live with her oldest daughter Lillie and husband, Sam. She deceased there. Her eulogy was at Center Ridge Baptist Church, and interment was in Center Ridge Cemetery. After she left the old home place, The house ran down and finally collapsed years after we all had moved away. Picture of the family house were not captured, during our stay on the farm. I wanted so much to put a picture in this book.

When grandmother deceased she had forty four grandchildren and host of great grands, and great great grand children. The Walker Family is a large family and widespread throughout the United States from California to Canada. Some of grandmother's land has been surveyed by her grand children that has an interest in keeping their parents part of the land for themselves.

CHAPTER X

An End and A New Beginning

"All's well that ends well; still the finish is the crown."Shakespeare
"Let us watch well our beginning, and results will manage themselves."

—Alex Clark

Migration was on the upswing and several southerners migrated from the South to the North in hope to find better jobs and economically live better lives. My little world began to change, childhood ended and a new beginning as an young adult.

After I joined Haywood in Hightstown, we begin our family. To this union three children were born: Miranda, John Douglas, and Leslie Mia Eutsey. Although Mia came along sixteen years later, after we moved to Trenton, New Jersey. All our three children were born in Princeton Medical Center, Princeton, New Jersey. We purchase our first home in Trenton, New Jersey in 1964. We stayed there in Trenton area for over thirty five years.

Grandmother and I wrote to each other, and I went back to visit her a few times. Times then, were kind of hard for us, having just married and started out on our own.

I did not get to visit her as much as I would have liked to, because we were so far apart and money was scarce. Let me share my last letter I received from her.

Birmingham 4 Ala
1637 Warrior Street
Feb 19, 1966

Dear Susie,

I received your letter and was glad to hear from you, glad to
hear that you and family Was well. This leaves me poorly. I
stays poorly all the time. I don't see a well day.

Lillie and Sam is well and doing all rite. It been mighty cool
there but the weather seems To be fair now I don't know
how long it will be this way.

It is pleasant now. Yes Susie come whenever you can get off.
I would like to see you and your family. I would be glad to
see you all. I hope the cool weather is over with.
I don't hardly ever see Adolph he is well though.

Your Grandmother,

Mary C. Walker

The postmark on the envelope stamped 21 February
1966. Sent to: Mrs. Susie Eutsey 841 Pennington Ave.,
Trenton, New Jersey 08618. Grandmother deceased the
next year

In March 1967. We drove from New Jersey to Mount Andrews,
Alabama for her funeral at Center Ridge Baptist Church.

As I move North, I quickly learned how to maneuver my way
through life. It like a sailboat you learn how to sail with the wind.
Wind that is blowing in the same direction as you are sailing is
actually not as favorable as one might think. Sometimes we need

to sail against the wind with sails under tension, while still maintaining your course.

Family life and church life can be a lot like sailing, there is always pressure of time and finances and plain old getting along. We can rejoice in those winds, knowing they produce perseverance, which produces character, and the product of character is hope.

Often we look back on life, we have some regrets. There are things we wish we have done. Like I did not apologize to grandmother for what I said to her or tell my sisters and brother I was sorry for what I did? I could have done something different when I was growing up, but not knowing any better at the time. And yet, there are some things for which we will never be sorry if we do them. (1) doing our best even when discouraged; (2) listen first and ask questions later; (3) spending time with our family; (4) standing by our principles in dealing with others; (5) asking forgiveness, even of our children, when wrong; (6) doing an honest days work to support our family; (7) reading to our children; (8) having family devotions. They have value and behavior are more "caught than taught." Action speaks louder than words.

The end of one year and the dawning of a new one provides an excellent opportunity to wipe the slate clean and make a fresh start. The well known preacher Henry Ward Beecher said "we have passed through one more year. One more long stage in the journey of life, with its ascents and descents and dust, mud, rocks thorns and burdens that wear the shoulders, is done. The old year is dead. Roll away. Let It go. God in his proficient, has brought us out of it. It is gone . . . Its evil has gone, It's the good remains. The evil has perished, and the good survives."

Look now back on yesterday, so full of failure and regrets. Look ahead and seek God's way—all sin confessed you must forget. Never let a dark past cloud a bright future. "forgetting those things which are behind and reaching forward to those things which are ahead—

Philippians 3:13" I must move forward with my life and focus on a new beginning.

Me and Haywood in Hightstown, NJ

When my first child was born I just had turned nineteen years old. With the second child I was twenty one, and when the third one was born I was thirty five years old. Sixteen years apart, what a "shock." The doctor said I would not have any more children, and I took his word. That was a new beginning, The dawn of information age.

EPILOGUE

As I look back over my life, a flood of memories surged over me as I remembered the farm, the family home place, where I spent my early childhood. I am intrigued by its multi-layered history and commitment of farm heroes of faith. Had I known that I would write this book earlier in life, more pictures would have been captured of the farm and family house. When we came on the scene, the farm was already in existence and seems to be functioning well. I left home after I married in 1948, and never lived there again. I only visited a few times. Finally it seem most the older people had died, the young people migrated North, and other places. Farming came to a stop, and Mount Andrews is now "defunct."

We have all moved away now, the land is still there, all grown up with trees, the family house, barn, shelters, and cribs, except one, have all caved in. The Magnolia tree still stand in the front yard, by where the gate was. The four of us took different directions in life. My brother Rozell live in Orlando, Florida with his family, our sister Ethel deceased, and Doreather live in Stone Mountain, Georgia with family and I live in Deltona, Florida with husband, and our youngest daughter Leslie along with two small children. Many of our first cousins and playmates have moved away to different parts of the United States from California, to Alaska. Grandmother and grandfather and all her eleven siblings have demised. My mother, father, and my oldest sister are deceased.

Many of our relatives, close friends, and playmates I talked about in my book have deceased. Some have moved back South. The Walker Family is a large family.

Now we have a family reunion each year in different states, this allow us to keep in contact and stay connected with both the older members and the new generation coming behind us.

As we move forward in the "new millennium," our agenda is set and we are focus on a "new beginning." We get to meet the new little people in our family. The Walker Family put on one of the best family reunion that I have seen or been too.

We have a banquet, and getting to know you, picnic, or fish fry. Our reunion always culminate with a service at one of the members church nearby. After church service, we have our Sunday Dinner at the church.

We have talented members, God have blessed us with speakers, preachers, teachers, singers, musicians, and the children put one outstanding show. I think God for my life, and the efforts that I have put into it, with his help. I have learned how to pull myself up by my own bootstraps. After my secondary education, I educated myself and always managed to keep a decent job. I am retired now, but I help to raised my two youngest grand children, Leroy Jr., and Latasha.

Printed in the United States
22156LVS00003B/18